Learning Citizenship

The Citizenship curriculum aims to help young people to participate more fully in society through the development of a range of relevant skills and knowledge. This book shows how a variety of teaching strategies can be used to teach citizenship skills across a range of curriculum subjects as well as in Citizenship lessons. Topics covered include:

- addressing controversial issues
- developing discussion
- thinking through debate
- investigating Citizenship
- learning through role play
- working in groups
- learning with simulations
- Citizenship in ICT
- participation.

This lively and practical book will be invaluable to student teachers and their trainers, Citizenship co-ordinators in school and advisers across the UK. It combines issues of pedagogy with real classroom experiences and demonstrates just how students learn from different teaching strategies. The book is full of case studies showing how Citizenship can be incorporated into a range of curriculum subjects.

Jenny Wales is currently Director of Education for Citizenship at the Nuffield Foundation and Chair of Examiners for Edexcel. **Paul Clarke** teaches Citizenship and general professional issues as well as Business and Economics to PGCE students at University College Worcester.

D1390433

Learning Citizenship

Practical teaching strategies
for secondary schools

Jenny Wales and Paul Clarke

RoutledgeFalmer
Taylor & Francis Group

LONDON AND NEW YORK

**The
Nuffield
Foundation**

First published 2005 by RoutledgeFalmer
2 Park Square, Milton Park, Abingdon, Oxfordshire, OX14 4RN

Simultaneously published in the USA and Canada
by RoutledgeFalmer
270 Madison Avenue, New York, NY 10016

RoutledgeFalmer is an imprint of the Taylor & Francis Group

© 2005 The Nuffield Foundation

Typeset in 10/12pt Goudy by
Graphicraft Limited, Hong Kong
Printed and bound in Great Britain by
TJ International Ltd, Padstow, Cornwall

British Library Cataloguing in Publication Data
A catalogue record for this book is available from the British Library

Library of Congress Cataloging in Publication Data
A catalog record for this book has been requested

ISBN 0-415-33534-5

Contents

Introduction

The objectives

Once Citizenship has become an integral part of the school curriculum, it provides opportunities for reflection on practice in the context of both the school and subject specialisms. For many, Citizenship provides a novel experience as it lends itself to a variety of teaching strategies which may be different from the norm in a range of subjects. Developing the skills required for debate, presentations, role play and group work, for example, help students to learn to build an argument – an asset in any subject.

The book aims to help the process of development and reflection by looking at practical experience of lessons in school combined with some underpinning theory. The initial two chapters of the book provide an overview of learning opportunities in Citizenship and a rationale for dealing with controversial issues. Subsequent chapters then each look at a specific teaching strategy and use a case study of a lesson or series of lessons to show how learning outcomes were achieved. Each one is full of examples of work and quotes from students demonstrating their achievement. The final two chapters deal with participation and whole school issues. These reflect the influence of key agencies including the Qualifications and Curriculum Authority (QCA) and the Office for Standards in Education (Ofsted) in the establishment of the subject.

Who will find the book useful?

Learning Citizenship provides support for a range of people in schools, higher education, local authorities and beyond:

- Citizenship co-ordinators
- Citizenship teachers both specialist and cross-curricular
- teachers in training
- teacher training lecturers
- advisers.

The combination of evidence from lessons, underpinning theory and reflection on the learning that has taken place, offers both fresh ideas and guidance for all concerned.

Citizenship plays a part in all teacher training courses and therefore provides a common theme for all students. The case studies may therefore also be useful to lecturers in general education when dealing with teaching strategies as they provide a common experience for students from all curriculum areas. This approach will also help trainees as many will find themselves asked to teach Citizenship at an early stage of their careers.

Using the book

Each teaching strategy is explored as a means of enhancing Citizenship teaching and contains a rationale for its use.

The case studies follow student thinking in a very practical way. They track each stage of the lesson and its outcomes.

The aims of each activity and a commentary on the context

Aims

- To draw together and apply learning on development issues.
- To develop the concept of voting.
- To develop discussion skills.

The school runs cross-curricular Citizenship and meets the requirements for global interdependence through Geography at Key Stage (KS) 4. There is a good fit between the two subjects on this topic and it offers opportunities to develop Citizenship skills.

A clear log of the stages of the lesson or series of lessons

The starter

The teacher introduced the lesson with a quick question-and-answer session to refresh memories about earlier work on development.

The activity takes about an hour so the introduction needs to be quick, or carried out in the previous lesson.

The core

Students watched the introductory part of the ICT-based simulation as a whole class and worked in pairs each time a decision was to be made. They then voted on what should be done. The whole class then discussed the decision and voted again to see if the discussion had changed people's views.

Each stage of the activity combined geographical knowledge and understanding with a growing facility with skills of debate, discussion and an appreciation of the democratic process. Students contributed willingly because they had rehearsed their arguments with a partner. They were required to justify their point of view and not just make a statement. The decision changed on several occasions as students listened to each other's point of view.

Examples of materials being used and sources for them

'President Mwlagi – we had to borrow money from abroad to rescue us from the situation we were in and to diversify our economy. Since taking out our loan we have managed to keep up with our interest repayments but haven't as yet managed to pay back any capital so we haven't reduced the principle debt . . .'

The advice is summed up on the screen:

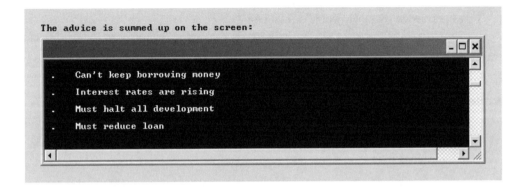

```
.   Can't keep borrowing money
.   Interest rates are rising
.   Must halt all development
.   Must reduce loan
```

Students' dialogue showing how their skills and understanding are developing

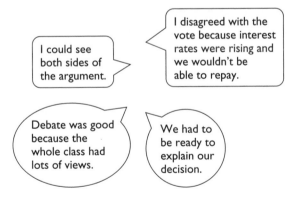

I could see both sides of the argument.

I disagreed with the vote because interest rates were rising and we wouldn't be able to repay.

Debate was good because the whole class had lots of views.

We had to be ready to explain our decision.

An analysis of the learning that has taken place

A student who says:

'I could see both sides of the argument.'

is clearly starting to deal with a range of perspectives and to appreciate that people have other points of view. It is a challenging and sophisticated skill to look at a problem from someone else's point of view. When a student says

'I was persuaded by other people's reasoning.'

the process is under way.

Reflection on the activity and its development

The KS3 Citizenship Scheme of Work Review Unit suggests that students should be asking questions like:

- What does this have to do with me?
- Do I have any responsibility?
- Is there anything I can do to influence the situation?

In this context it is important to work out with the Geography teacher how responding to such questions can contribute to the subject.

Strategies across the curriculum

Ideas for the teaching strategies in other subject areas help provide ideas and guidance for teachers involved in Citizenship.

Questions for reflection

Questions for reflection aim to help teachers in practice and training to consider issues related to each strategy. They are of use to co-ordinators and advisers for the development of training sessions.

Chapter 1

Reflective teaching, reflective learning

Thinking about Citizenship

Teaching Citizenship is often different from any mainstream subject experience. In the National Curriculum, Citizenship appears as a discrete heading. It expects schools to provide students with opportunities for participation as well as the knowledge and skills components; and it asks them to develop whole school programmes. It is therefore formalising many of the things that schools already do and asking them to incorporate them into a Citizenship framework.

Some schools already have well-established programmes and the National Curriculum guidance offers some clear links to subject Programmes of Study. Personal, social and health education (PSHE) and Citizenship Units of Work are offered on national websites to support specialist Citizenship lessons through the Key Stages. The decisions to be made are about 'where' and 'when' to teach particular aspects of citizenship.

Schools are using a wide range of strategies, both across the curriculum and within specific subject areas, which take into account students' experiences in different school and community contexts. This book suggests ways in which a range of activities can be tried and developed in different contexts in schools in order to create a successful whole school strategy. Different chapters show how teachers have worked in and across subject classrooms to explore Citizenship with their students.

The process of reflection-in-action (Schon 1983) requires a thoughtful approach, some systematic use of evidence about students' learning and time together with others to explore the issues. Some of the factors that contribute to reflection in action and a thoughtful approach are:

- sharing an interest in Citizenship activities and their consequences for the school community
- being open-minded, responsible and whole-hearted (Dewey 1916) about Citizenship
- recognising the value of reviewing their own practice, using evidence from classroom enquiry and other research
- enjoying collaboration and dialogue with teaching colleagues
- looking for creativity in the development of teaching and learning strategies for Citizenship.

Key questions for reflection

There are masses of resources for the classroom and extra-curricular activities to support Citizenship (National Curriculum 2003) but making the best use of them requires a thoughtful approach on the part of individual teachers and Citizenship co-ordinators. Chapters in this book provide ideas for using such resources to develop different kinds of Citizenship skills and understanding in students. Later chapters look at strategies for working together across school and beyond school to encourage more active participation on the part of students in both their school and local communities.

Reflection means asking thoughtful questions about what is happening in the classroom and beyond. The questions are familiar to all in the context of existing subject teaching.

- What do I want students to learn?
- How can I ensure thoughtful learning?
- How can I find out what students actually learn?
- How does Citizenship learning in my class fit with learning elsewhere?
- How can I work with other teachers to answer these questions?

Each chapter ends with some questions and tasks which are designed to help teachers to apply the ideas in the case studies to their own schools.

Active learning

In preparing students for Citizenship, school experiences must help to shape their future action and help them to make sense of new ideas. This can be achieved through active learning that helps students to draw on their previous experiences in order to understand and evaluate new ideas. It involves making new ideas accessible (Bruner 1966) by relating them to students' previous experiences and providing carefully constructed steps or scaffolding to support learning.

Students at John Cabot School in Bristol, where Citizenship is incorporated into Information and Communication Technology (ICT), were trying to understand why the plight of asylum seekers caused so much debate. They had little knowledge of the reasons why people were seeking asylum in the United Kingdom so they were guided through an investigation using the BBC website. In the process they became more informed about individual stories and the changing numbers of applications from selected countries. Students were asked to create an informative leaflet of the kind sent out to the public by a government. They had to exercise selection skills because the word count was limited

Developing the scaffolding in Citizenship

Asylum seekers in an ICT lesson

Staging of experiences:

- start with case study of a young asylum seeker's story with strong narrative
- emphasis on empathy
- use data from website to broaden understanding; how typical are these people of asylum seekers; more objectivity expected
- write a summary report for a given audience; requiring higher order skills.

and to try to understand how asylum issues were seen by a government rather than by an individual. Finally, they were invited to express their views to their local Member of Parliament (MP) via email links made in an earlier unit of work. The learning embraced knowledge, skills and participation.

Activity means 'do and review'

Doing, reviewing, learning and applying (Kolb 1984) highlights the importance of activity to

- engage students
- encourage reflection
- extract and evaluate meaning
- applying the learning to future thoughts and deeds.

The National Strategies (Department for Education and Skills (DfES) 2003), which aim to improve the quality of teaching and learning at KS3, illustrates how such learning principles can be translated into lesson planning with starters, challenging activities and plenaries. A historian in Lacon Childe School (see Chapter 4) applied these principles in teaching his students some rudimentary debating skills. An initial phase asked students to recap on their knowledge from a previous lesson about progress resulting from the industrial revolution in Britain. He invited them to debate as two halves of the class and created rules for argument and counter-argument. Students were challenged to use evidence to debate the case. A plenary session asked students to think about how they had tackled the task, to identify appropriate skills and to think how they might find evidence if the debate took place in contemporary Britain.

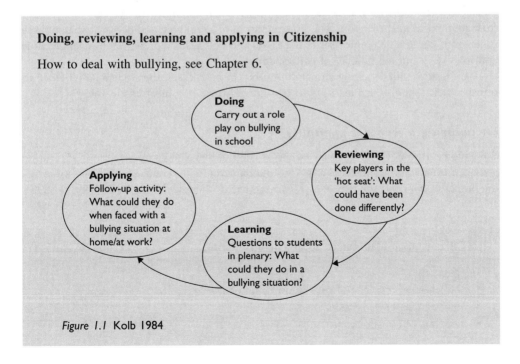

Doing, reviewing, learning and applying in Citizenship

How to deal with bullying, see Chapter 6.

Figure 1.1 Kolb 1984

Looking for meaning

The focus of learning should involve a search for a deep, rather than a surface, meaning. Students who view learning to be about memorising and reproducing knowledge, tackle a task very differently from those who view learning to be about seeing things in a different way (Marton 1981). Future citizens may have a need to recall information on the spot, but they also need to see issues from different perspectives and begin to examine their own ideas in different ways. Without such education, it is hard to imagine how young citizens would make sense of the reporting of wars and the reasons why governments of some nations send their troops to fight.

Large-scale and small-scale tasks

The national guidelines for Citizenship expect students at the end of KS3 to be able to understand how the public gets its information and how opinions can be formed and expressed. The KS4 programme expects students to understand something of the ways in which political and economic systems work. Good contexts within and across curriculum subjects provide a meaningful framework for important, complex and controversial issues.

The Campaign, an investigation in Chapter 5, illustrates how students move from a classroom-based activity towards a research task focused on the working of local councils and pressure groups. The investigation runs over several lessons and forms a substantial Citizenship unit within the PSHE programme.

In contrast, an English teacher in Christopher Whitehead School, in Chapter 6, succeeds in challenging students to think again about their views of bullying through a role play which is self-contained within one or two subject lessons. Students find much satisfaction in pursuing an issue in detail and with real commitment because that is what they are used to in this lesson. The interpretation of 'economic and political system' here is generous because a complex set of decisions and policies is represented by a single issue and involves a limited number of participants.

These lessons differ in scale and ambition but in both cases, the students are helped to transfer their school-based learning to real-life contexts in a meaningful way.

Encouraging a 'can do' mentality

Students need to develop a positive view of their achievements and to avoid attributing poor performance to themselves as a kind of character fault. The negative effect of focusing on performance at the expense of learning leaves them feeling helpless (Butler 1998).

In Citizenship students need to be encouraged to:

- have a go
- believe that they can always improve and learn
- take on challenging tasks
- ask lots of questions.

If they believe that they have to be clever before they can tackle a task, and if they feel that they must always appear clever in front of their peers and teachers, they will be less successful learners.

Chapter 5 explains how Rhodesway School in Bradford used *The Campaign* as a basis for a Citizenship investigation. Some students decided to deal directly with the local mayor on the phone to find out local government plans.

One school asked a technology group to take on a 'commission' from a business partner to design decorations for a special Halloween event in a restaurant. The students were not all confident in their own ability to be creative, to manage the process of plastic injection moulding, nor to complete a task in a given time limit. A visit from the restaurant manager provided a real fillip because they were expected to succeed and they realised the business was serious about using their ideas. At the end of a series of lessons involving starts and false starts, two groups presented their finished prototypes and were delighted to receive orders from the business manager. They were less pleased when he asked them to tone down their ideas for scary masks and green-coloured cheese in the interests of keeping his customers. The students' self-esteem was boosted but an important lesson was learned about researching the needs of a client.

Valuing different kinds of learners

Future citizens will be encountering new ideas in many different ways. In later life they will be valued for their ability to communicate, their sensitivity to others as well as academic qualities. The intelligent learner comes in many different forms and it is important to value their different characteristics. Both multiple intelligences (Gardner 1999) and emotional intelligence (Goleman 1995) have contributed to an understanding of how young people learn and interact (Figure 1.2).

When considering the education of the whole child (Rogers 1961) it is clear that feelings are an important part of the process of learning. Thinking about the affective

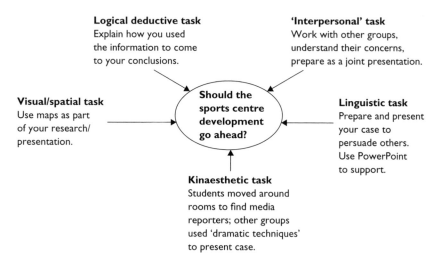

Figure 1.2

domain can be as powerful as cognitive development and may be at the heart of a worth-while Citizenship activity.

In one school assembly, a visiting representative from Christian Aid expressed his anger at the apparent arrogance of some people who assumed they were solving all the problems of 'deprived' families in Africa by making financial donations. The strong emotions on show generated much debate in the school where regular collections for charities were an assumed part of life. Students began to ask questions about what money was collected, for whom and why.

In another school, Year 7 students were asked about the progress they thought they had made in the development of Citizenship skills in the past year. Several students described how a group of girls had provided brilliant support for other students who were worried about bullying, about their lack of confidence and about their own personal relationships. The girls' interactive skills were highly prized by students and their views have encouraged school governors and staff to review the provision of counselling and welfare support in the school.

In Chapter 6, it is clear that the impact of a role play on the participants was strengthened by the commitment and feelings expressed about bullying. While teachers have to exercise care in managing the activity and ensure that the students are helped out of role at the end of the lesson, the experience is likely to stay in students' minds for a long time. It may also help students to transfer their learning from school to home where serious issues are discussed. Feelings often run high in such situations and it is important that students can manage to mix passion with more measured argument.

Learning together

It is hard to imagine how any young citizen could learn effectively about rights and responsibilities alone with just a book and a quiet room. Social interaction makes an important contribution to good learning (Bruner 1996; Vygotsky 1978). A school setting is an obvious place where students can test out their understanding of what it means to take responsibility for their behaviour and that of others. They can voice different ideas about rights and wrongs and learn that their perspectives on life may be different to those of others around them (Figure 1.3).

Group activity is a feature of many Citizenship activities and as is evident at the Ridgeway School (see Chapter 11), students can be effective co-teachers as well as co-learners. Students as well as teachers can help learners to discover or understand ideas in a way that was just beyond them as individuals (Vygotsky 1978). The insight provided by students to the class at Ridgeway School led them to look at the situation in a very different way. One teacher can have an impact on the thinking of a whole class but students as teachers can orchestrate as effective an impact in a different way within a small group or whole class activity.

Talking constructively

The unpredictable nature of discussion and of students' behaviour can be a worry to teachers unused to managing lessons based on a lot of interaction among students. Care-fully constructed simulations are one solution because they can lead students to discuss sensitive issues in a way which can be managed successfully while still giving room for

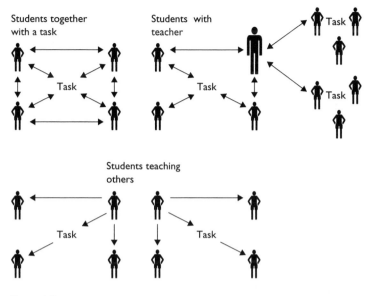

Students together with a task

Students with teacher

Task

Task

Task

Task

Students teaching others

Task

Task

Figure 1.3

personal expression. In Chapter 9, *President for a Day* helps students to understand the issues relating to economic development in an African country. They are presented with contradictory evidence for different decisions and therefore have to evaluate and come to conclusions themselves.

Students' communication skills lie at the heart of social interaction and Chapter 3 illustrates the importance of discussion to Citizenship development. There is evidence from classrooms that students often experience 'discussion' in practice as a question-and-answer session with the teacher asking all the questions (Dillon 1994). At Tunbridge Wells Boys' Grammar School, the teacher has placed students in the position of asking the questions of each other as much as of herself. The exchange of views between students is prompted by well-designed tasks and resources and supported by the occasional intervention from a teacher.

The quality of the discussion is obviously important. It is unlikely that students' understanding of crime and punishment will be developed by a version of 'pub talk' where a student with one view about imprisonment attempts to shout down another with a different view. The development of 'thoughtfulness' in students allows them to express their own view, to recognise that other people may hold different perspectives, and to set out to look at the similarities and differences between their views and those of others (Newmann 1990). An example of this thoughtfulness at work can be seen in Chapter 8, where students were asked to make presentations to put their point of view on the development of a football stadium and the provision of sports facilities. They had to decide on the factors that would support their argument most effectively and create a persuasive presentation. Their brief included working out the questions that were most likely to be posed by other members of the class so that they would be better prepared to deal with challenges from other people with different points of view.

Time for reflection

The importance of well-directed reflection on group activity and social interaction is crucial to good learning. Students' ability to learn from situations is enhanced when they are asked *how* they learned as well as *what* they learned (Shayer and Adey 1994). Some materials developed as part of the KS3 Strategy to improve teaching and learning stress the importance of thinking about thinking or metacognition.

Students who had worked on *The Campaign* (see Chapter 5) were asked to explain how they arrived at their ideas for developing a new leisure centre in their community. One group described how they had designed a questionnaire and collected the views of a range of local residents; another had interviewed a well-known and much respected local councillor; a third group had discussed ideas among themselves and had arrived at a ranking of teenagers' own priorities. The whole class was asked to consider how effective the different approaches had been and to offer advice to a group that was about to begin the exercise. The quality of their responses was impressive and suggests that future citizens can be sensitive to other people's concerns as well as aware of some of the political processes involved in local decision-making.

Quality learning in Citizenship

The principles behind these accounts of teaching and learning will not be new to many teachers who believe effective teaching processes involve:

- active learning
- collaborative learning
- responsibility in learning
- learning about learning.

The interpretation of these principles in the context of Citizenship is new and this book aims to offer some guidance for their incorporation into Citizenship programmes in schools.

In subjects where discussion, for example, is a strength of classroom work, the question to be explored by teachers is about the quality of Citizenship learning evident in the outcomes of the discussion. What is the impact of a debate in science about recycling products such as plastic shopping bags, a review of a technology project on effective ways of carrying heavy shopping loads and of a geography investigation of the siting of a new supermarket?

Citizenship in and out of school

Another issue for discussion in school is the best context for effective Citizenship teaching and learning. It is helpful to plan explicit lessons on aspects of Citizenship knowledge and skills when it is clear that students have little prior knowledge on which they can draw. But there is a case for arguing that the learning will be most meaningful for students if it is set in real contexts in which students are actively engaged. A group of students tussling with the problem of how best to get their whole year group to agree on a fundraising activity has a real need to find out about voting processes or about good leadership skills.

Again, a Citizenship issue brought into school by students has the advantages of extra motivation, of real ownership of tasks, and the possibility of offering lots of different kinds of involvement. On the other hand, the ambition and scale of ventures can often be managed more successfully inside a classroom and the learning outcomes may be clearer to all.

Chapters 11 and 12 offer some guidance on different approaches that may be adopted by teachers and by Citizenship co-ordinators to the choice of contexts inside and across classrooms.

Questions for reflection

- Identify a topic which you enjoy teaching as part of your subject work. How do you make it interesting and meaningful to your students?
- How could you use these strategies to teach an aspect of Citizenship?
- How do your teaching and learning strategies for Citizenship compare with those of your colleagues?
- In what ways could aspects of your subject work help your students as citizens outside school?

Chapter 2

Reflective teaching and controversial issues

What is a controversial issue?

An issue is controversial if a substantial number of people disagree about its substance or assumptions. Such issues are at the heart of Citizenship because they are underpinned by values and beliefs that divide people at local, national and international levels. The Programme of Study asks young people to express their own opinions but appreciate that others have different points of view.

> **The Citizenship Programme of Study on controversial issues**
>
> - research a topical political, spiritual, moral, social or cultural issue, problem or event
> - express, justify and defend orally and in writing a personal opinion about such issues, problems or events
> - use their imagination to consider other people's experiences and be able to think about, express, explain and critically evaluate views that are not their own.
>
> (QCA 2002)

Controversial issues include those that have been in the public domain for a long time such as euthanasia, equality for homosexuals, fair trade, asylum seekers or environmental protection. They may divide the nation and be the very focus of political and moral debate.

Local issues can stimulate as much, or even more, controversy when alternative views are advocated with an equal amount of passion.

Local planning proposals, which involve extending roads and runways, building large superstores, resiting a hospital or closing a school, can all cause a furore. To some extent, it is possible to see controversy in almost anything that is rooted in a particular set of values.

Why deal with controversial issues?

It is tempting to shy away from such issues in school for a number of reasons.

- They can appear to be difficult to manage because of the need to be fair and sensitive to students from different backgrounds and with differing views.
- Dealing with confrontation can be challenging.
- The fear of exposing young people to the harsh controversies of adult life at too early a stage in their lives.

The Crick (1998) report on Citizenship is unambiguous on this front: 'Education . . . should prepare children to deal with such controversies knowledgeably, sensibly, tolerantly and morally'.

The inclusion of controversial issues in the curriculum encourages some positive outcomes for Citizenship. These include the development of critical thinking and interpersonal skills (Harwood and Hahn 1990) and increased levels of political interest, confidence and social integration (Soley 1996).

The Citizenship Programme of Study expects . . .

Not only does the Citizenship Programme of Study ask students to acquire skills related to controversial issues, but also it provides a wide range of contexts to investigate. These include diversity, the role of the media, ways in which conflicts can be resolved and global issues and events. Students are expected to think about topical issues and to express and justify opinions, to learn how to consider the experiences of others, and to take part responsibly in activities. Controversial issues, therefore, cannot be ignored.

There are many examples in later chapters which illustrate ways of tackling such issues in the classroom.

- An opportunity for thoughtful discussion in Mathematics in Chapter 3 encourages students to express opinions knowledgeably and to consider the implications and uses of a range of statistical evidence.
- Debating skills encourage students to counter views and to weigh up evidence from different sources; the case study of a History lesson in Chapter 4 shows how students use evidence from the past to frame a debate about the nature of individual and community freedom.
- The investigation in Chapter 5 shows how students delved deeply into a local issue from a number of different perspectives and developed persuasive arguments in their reports.
- In Chapter 6 a class develops skills of empathy and students handle the sensitive issue of bullying with tolerance by placing themselves in 'other people's shoes'.
- In Chapter 10 students are asked to find information about asylum seekers in order to create a leaflet giving people a clear picture of the facts.

Bias and balance

There are guidelines that are intended to make the teaching and learning of controversial issues more straightforward. Many are designed to preserve a degree of 'balance' between different views and to deal with bias, on the part of teachers and students.

The Education Act 1996 forbids the promotion of partisan political views in school and will allow only students of 12 and over to take part in political activities while at school. Teachers are expected to take reasonable steps to offer balanced presentations or opposing views.

Citizenship guidance (QCA 2002) identifies ways in which teachers can avoid bias.

- Give all evidence equal emphasis.
- Make it clear that information is always open to interpretation.
- Do not appear to be the sole authority on matters of 'fact' and opinion.
- Use the actual claims of groups as source and not a teacher's paraphrasing.
- Use 'neutral' body language.
- Give all students equal opportunity to contribute their views.
- Challenge easily arrived-at opinions or consensus views.

Such lists can deter those who feel less than superhuman but do provide useful targets to work towards in planning and teaching. A raised eyebrow, when used in response to one student's view and not to another, can be very significant. Above all else, indoctrination of students must be avoided.

Many schools have a particular stance on some issues such as racism and discrimination. The prevailing ethos is clear to all members of a school community and everyone will recognise that not all actions, attitudes and views are equally acceptable. Other sources of guidance lie within the school as teaching about values already occurs in English, Humanities and Science lessons among other departments.

QCA guidance suggests that when dealing with controversial issues, students should learn how to recognise bias and how to evaluate evidence and different interpretations. But above all else, students should be able to give good reasons for everything they say and do.

It is not difficult to think of examples of how this could be put into practice.

- A variety of source materials containing different kinds of biased language based on different perspectives.
- Writing frames to encourage students to record not only the solution they have chosen but also the reason why.
- A task that asks students to prioritise ideas and give their reasons.
- A summarising exercise after a debate where students record different views and identify the extent to which they are counter-arguments.

Students often use emotions as well as reason to determine actions (Ashton and Watson 1998). Rational proofs and careful deduction are often lacking in moral controversy when emotion becomes involved. Students need to exhibit an active desire to value, appreciate, listen to and interact with the views of others using both reasoning and feelings. They need to be able to reflect on these views, and where appropriate incorporate them into their understanding and beliefs.

This approach carries an important assumption about learning. Students are not simply 'collecting knowledge' or developing 'reasoning skills'. They are evaluating how they and others perceive and feel about the world and their place in it. At its most ambitious level, learning changes who we are and how we operate in the world (Marton 1981). This idea sits comfortably with the aim of Citizenship programmes to prepare students for the adult world and to take part in and to improve decision-making processes.

Planning for controversial issues

There are three aspects of planning lessons on controversial issues which require particular care:

- selecting study materials
- dealing with teachers' own perspectives
- planning for students' participation.

Selecting study materials

The Key Stages 3 and 4 Citizenship programmes provide a broad framework but leave the detail of what to teach and how to teach it for practitioners. In deciding on materials and a context for Citizenship lessons or units of work, there is freedom to make judgements that will reflect individual priorities and those of the school.

The exemplar materials on QCA's website include a range of activities which involve controversial contexts. These exemplars are useful but decisions still need to be made about the best way to use them given the time constraints in school.

Contexts that are meaningful and interesting help students to think about the big issues within and beyond the local environment. There are various ways of achieving this.

- When students select their own issues the added familiarity increases their motivation.
- Materials that challenge students to think about multicultural or global issues can excite interest even if they are less familiar and take longer to understand.
- Issues which can be presented in two dramatically opposed versions challenge students to think about their own positions. With younger students, it can be helpful to present relatively 'simple' and 'clear' dilemmas to help discussion when they are at an early stage in their moral and logical development.

(Kibble 1998)

Whatever the choices, contexts may need to be revised frequently if students are to be given the chance to study topical issues.

A BBC radio poll invited listeners to recommend a law which they would most like to see introduced. Top of the list was the suggestion that citizens should be able to use any means to defend their property against burglars and thieves. This might be an interesting stimulus for discussion in the context of law-making and could be seen as a safe issue distanced from students' immediate experience. However, it could soon become a hot potato if a local case hit the headlines and it could take a lot of class time to research the background to the BBC poll, to find out the views of the school community, and to discover the detail of current laws or proposals for change.

Dealing with teachers' own perspectives

All teachers involved in Citizenship have their own perspectives on issues and they have to work out how to deal with them in the context of the classroom. There is a range of alternative strategies to choose from but it helps to make a clear decision about the one selected and be aware of the issues related to each strategy.

Procedural neutrality

Procedural neutrality (Stenhouse 1983) is best exemplified by the idea of a 'neutral chair-person' who manages classroom debates. It avoids the risk of imposing views on a class and works well when a lot of learning support materials are available. Evaluators of Stenhouse's (1970) *The Humanities Project* reported that it proved to be a difficult position to sustain. The 'neutrality' threatened rapport with classes and appeared to cast doubts on a teacher's personal credibility. Even body language communicated a view when trying to talk in a neutral fashion. It has been suggested that it is nonsensical for the most experienced person in the room not to get involved, especially when ill-informed views are being expressed (Ashton and Watson 1998).

Impartial approach

An impartial approach can be adopted when presenting information so all sides of an argument are covered without revealing a personal view. This is clearly helpful when there is much conflicting information and when a balanced range of views does not come from a group of students. It can also show that issues are not two-dimensional. However, there are different views about 'balance' and the approach can lead to too much teacher direction in the lesson.

Playing devil's advocate

Playing devil's advocate involves consciously adopting a particular position to present to students. This can be helpfully provocative to a group, especially when they all appear to share a particular view. It runs the risk of students believing the views to be those held by the teacher and it may also reinforce students' prejudices. In one lesson, a teacher outlined a racist view that blamed ethnic minorities for rising unemployment in the area. He subjected the view to criticism using a range of statistics but some students could recall only the view, not the criticism, at a later date. Some parents complained to the school about the teacher's apparently 'racist' views. It is therefore important to ensure that students are aware of the strategy and for it to be used in different contexts.

A stated commitment

A stated commitment (Kelly 1986) means providing a range of views on an issue but also sharing personal views with the class. As students are likely to try to guess these personal views anyway, it seems sensible to share the view and help students to spot any likely prejudices or bias which result. It presents the teacher as a human being who acts upon reasoned convictions and provides a role model. This strategy must be treated with care because students who find it difficult to sort fact from opinion may, of course, find it harder if the two are embodied in the same person, their teacher. They may also find it difficult to argue against such opinions and just go with the flow.

   Using a range of approaches in different situations makes it possible to respond to particular issues effectively and helps students to understand how people mediate controversial topics in other aspects of life.

Planning for students' participation

Facilitating participation needs practice and one way of doing this is to create a participative environment in the classroom. Lessons in which students have to make choices help them to develop the skills they need for bigger forms of participation. It is, however, worth bearing in mind that flexibility is important and contingency plans may be needed to deal with their choices. The route they choose may be more time-consuming so if achieving a given amount of subject content is critical, the trade-offs need to be considered. On the positive side, the gains from the experience may create more efficient learning in future.

If students are to become actively involved in an issue on their own terms, there may be some unexpected or unwanted outcomes for the school. In a school that encouraged enterprise activities among a whole range of year groups, teachers were pleased to see a venture where students sold healthier food snacks at break time. Unfortunately, a related fall in sales of products from catering staff led to the loss of a part-time job. Not surprisingly, there were complaints that the enterprise was poorly prepared and gave students priority over catering staff. Discussion at the planning stage may have avoided criticism later about bias and balance from other members of the school community.

Another group of students were involved in the planning of an English project about school publicity materials. Some chose to develop a new brochure for feeder primary schools and were very concerned to be honest about their own secondary school; they wanted to 'tell it how it really was'. They included material on how little bullying there was in the school and how well it was handled by the staff and students. When they took the brochure to a primary school, some Year 6 pupils were very worried because bullying was mentioned, and the English teacher was concerned that the wrong message had been given to prospective students and their parents. It is a good idea to involve teachers and possibly governors in the planning stage of activities which have a high public profile to avoid any misunderstandings. There are also tough decisions to take about the extent to which students should share responsibility for decisions involving them in the world beyond the school that may be controversial.

Teaching controversial issues

Students need to learn how to reflect and think for themselves, so it is important to use teaching strategies that allow them to explore ideas.

Discussion

Discussion is an effective strategy but requires careful structure and practice if students are to avoid indulgence and an 'exchange of ignorance'. Court trials offer one particular model and a 'fair hearing of competing views' is a useful framework to use in a classroom. Younger students can be encouraged to try communicating their views through a regular 'taking a stand' exercise. Chapter 3 contains a case study of Year 7 students using an assortment of data in Mathematics to explore the structure of the UK population. The students worked in groups to discuss the meaning of the data and its potential use. Discussion showed that they were surprised by the evidence when compared with their personal perceptions.

Role-playing and simulations

Role-playing and simulations can stimulate debate about controversial issues and provide an opportunity to explore other people's perspectives. The case study in Chapter 6 describes how students explore different views on bullying and how they react to being placed in 'the hot seat' at the end of the lesson. In Chapter 9 students challenge the very basis of 'development' and who it benefits as part of a Geography simulation. The seriousness with which they take on the 'simulated world' created by the teacher and the resource reflects their commitment and responsibility and draws out some real feelings as well as reasoning.

Many role-play lessons on controversial issues are the better for using third-party examples to ensure students talk about other people's experiences but still feel able to voice their own opinion. English teachers are well aware of the advantage of a good piece of literature for this purpose and cite the well-known example of 'walking around in other people's shoes' in *To Kill a Mockingbird* (Lee 1960).

It can be difficult to stand in someone else's shoes in a role play. However, an attempt may encourage an individual to accommodate new ideas and thus begin to change his or her worldview. The attempt to help students to 'balance' their own view against that of another may be more important than pursuing a 'balance' of all the different views which exist.

Critical investigation

Critical investigation can help students to explore emotionally charged issues in a series of steps known as a 'demystification strategy' (Clarke 1992) using these key questions.

- What is the issue about? Values? Information? Definitions?
- What are the arguments?
- What is assumed?
- How are the arguments manipulated?

The Campaign described in Chapter 5 is based on students investigating how a local leisure centre proposal might benefit different groups. Students present 'solutions' to the whole class in preparation for a vote on the 'best' idea. Different groups not only have to research appropriate information but also learn how to shape the material to persuade others to think in the same way. Students are encouraged to think about possible causes and consequences of their decisions throughout by briefing sheets and by teacher prompts.

Some schools have involved local politicians in such investigations to provide authentic voices and to give status and self-esteem for students who feel that young people's views are not taken seriously. The need for students to have a good armoury of critical questions becomes even more important when 'adult experts' are involved.

Students might ask:

- How do you know? (The nature of evidence)
- From whose viewpoint is this being presented? (A matter of perspective)
- Why is this important? (Relevance)

A disquieting feature of some investigations is that students (and teachers) have to work with incomplete evidence or obviously biased sources. Students investigating the expansion of a limestone quarry as part of a science and society activity were faced with large quantities of glossy booklets supplied by the quarrying industry and very little data on the environmental impact of quarrying on local communities. A mock 'public inquiry' gave insight into the rules used to decide such issues but many students were uneasy at having to make a judgement with such partial information. This could be viewed as a successful experience in that some students were more critical of those who rush to judgement. While some students would have been happier with more 'complete answers', there is no need for concern if at the end, students have more questions to investigate than when they began.

Thoughtful students

Controversial issues are easier to manage when students are used to a culture of thoughtful reflection (Newmann 1990). Newmann uses the label of 'thoughtfulness' to describe students who expect all claims to be backed by reason, who have a tendency to be reflective rather than impulsive and show curiosity and flexibility in their thinking. Teachers need to strike a balance between the development of knowledge, the right kind of attitudes and appropriate skills. A way of approaching this is to encourage students to develop and test their thinking in non-routine situations.

These characteristics of thoughtfulness were observed in one Mathematics classroom, where the teacher was keen to see students think for themselves as often as possible. A poster on the wall promoted the 4Bs.

Use your **Brain**
Ask a **Buddy**
Look in a **Book**
Ask the **Boss**

When a student asked how long was a metre, the class was asked to put up their hands and show a 'guestimate' of a metre to each other. It was an expectation that everyone should be able to have a rough idea of quantities, or units, so that any calculation could be quickly double-checked for accuracy.

As part of a Year 10 activity, students were asked to 'investigate' a problem that had appeared in a local paper. 'How best to cover the costs of health services in a way that was fair to everyone?' In particular, how should emergency services be paid for? Ambulances and hospitals were based in one large conurbation in the county and a service had to reach small outlying villages as well as the many thousands of households just a short distance away in the city.

Students worked in groups prompted by a picture of an accident and an outline map of the county. They discussed the string of consequences that might arise from a motoring accident in several different locations. They drew on their prior knowledge of other circumstances in which costs of services are paid by the users or shared by the community.

Students were not afraid to tackle an unfamiliar problem because they were routinely asked to think about the nature of the problem and not just to practise calculations. The ambulance problem asked students to think about the variables relevant to the task as well as to make calculations when some variables changed. Students had developed the knowledge, the attitudes and some skills that allowed them to use their Mathematics to tackle economic and political issues important to Citizenship.

Deciding what to teach and how to teach it depends to a large extent on the knowledge of the students. While pre-testing of students' knowledge is commonplace it is equally important to find out their attitudes and opinions (Lynch and McKenna 1990). Such information can be used to group students and for planning differentiated activities. Attitudes and beliefs can also be retested at the end to detect changes.

Questions for reflection

Think about your own teaching:

- To what extent do you plan to teach about controversial issues?
- Do such issues arise unexpectedly in other settings?
- What do you do if a student asks for your opinion on an issue?
- How do you find out about your students' prior knowledge, attitudes and values?
- How do you help students to examine each other's viewpoints and reasoning?

Investigate other teachers' approaches:

- Find out how other teachers tackle one issue important to all of you.
- Observe and discuss how a particular episode is handled in a lesson.

Chapter 3

Developing discussion

Why use discussion?

Discussion has been at the heart of education for thousands of years. It helps learning because it encourages students to voice opinions and support their point of view in a group so ideas are shared and developed. Members of the group have to learn to listen to other people's perspectives and ideas, consider them and respond. This is a central aspect of the skills that the Citizenship Programme of Study expects young people to develop.

At both KS3 and KS4, they should be able to 'contribute to group and exploratory class discussions' and at KS4 they are asked to 'express, justify and defend orally and in writing a personal opinion about such issues, problems or events'.

In some subjects, discussion is a common occurrence but in others, when contributions are made to the Citizenship curriculum, it is important to consider the nature of the learning that is taking place. The case study in this chapter is drawn from Mathematics. The lesson involves the use and purpose of data and shows how the development of these skills adds to mathematical understanding as well as helping students to look at the structure of the UK population including age, religion and ethnicity. Discussion in any subject is most effective when the class becomes a community of inquiry (Lipman 2003) in which each student participates in a group or whole class discussion.

Discussion is always more than just chatting because it addresses a serious matter and aims to develop a deeper understanding of the problem or issue. The skills that are learnt from discussion can enhance understanding in many areas, both in and out of school. It can lead young people to question the tabloid headline approach that is so frequently used by people to express their point of view. Even if not actually involved in real discussion at the time, young people can begin to realise the difference between just stating a view and being prepared to justify and defend it.

Running discussions

The right environment

Discussion needs to take place in a quiet, calm environment. This can be difficult to achieve in school, so it is worth considering whether one lesson of the week meets these requirements rather than another. It may be better to choose a time when the students haven't just come from Physical Education (PE) or are in the room where the school buses draw up outside in readiness for the end of the day.

In order to create a community of inquiry, students involved in discussion need to be able to focus clearly on the development of ideas. If members of a class are working on different activities, it may be hard for group discussion to take place because of the potential disruption from people doing other things. Discussion is therefore best carried out when the class is involved, either in groups or as a whole.

There is no best structure for discussion as it depends on the class itself. In small groups, the structure is straightforward because three, four or five students can sit in a circle and converse easily. As a whole class, there is a range of alternatives.

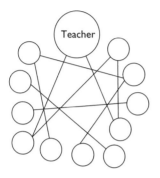

Figure 3.1 A Matrix

- A formal structure can be used in which students sit in rows facing the teacher. This has the drawback that they expect a more didactic approach when seated in this fashion and may be less willing to participate in genuine dialogue. It also means that they cannot see each other's faces and much learning takes place from watching the responses of others.
- A matrix in which the teacher is facilitator is effective because everyone sits as a group and can see, hear and respond to each other. It does however leave a large open space in the centre that can intimidate some and inspire others to perform.

Learning to discuss effectively in small groups is probably most effective because it overcomes the issues of working as a large group. It encourages students to feel at ease and not expect a more didactic approach than the teacher is intending. Even when discussion is the objective, student expectations can divert the plans because they are used to a different approach. It is therefore useful to change the physical environment of students to overcome the habits that they have developed.

The role of the teacher

Students and teachers have expectations of each other's behaviour so careful strategies have to be used to encourage discussion in an environment in which it is not the most common classroom activity. Students are used to teachers being the providers of information and the givers of credit for right answers.

Even when planning to discuss, it is easy, when interacting with a group, to contribute more than other members of the group, so it is important to consider ways of ensuring that students' contributions make up about 80 per cent of the time available. This will mean devising a strategy so students know that the rules have changed. Spending a little time drawing up the rules with the group as a whole is one way of doing this. It fits particularly well into the context of Citizenship because it develops an understanding of why we need rules and what makes rules fair. The rules may cover:

- speaking
- listening
- taking turns
- recording what is being said
- drawing conclusions and justifying them.

In the discussion itself, a group needs a facilitator to co-ordinate and administer the rules. This role can be taken by the teacher but may also be carried out by a student. It is good practice for students to do this in turns because they start to realise the issues involved in letting everyone have their say and being certain that points are justified, so people are not making unsupported inputs. They are more likely to gain useful experience by taking this role in a small group initially.

Encouraging students to take the role of facilitator can also leave the teacher free to play the role of contributor. When a group comes to a tricky issue or needs an input of evidence that they do not have, the teacher can be drawn in to help. If each group is functioning effectively, the teacher can circulate and be drawn in as necessary.

Strategies for encouraging discussion

- Sitting at the same level as the students.
- Taking turns to talk.
- Using a means of identifying whose turn it is such as a symbolic microphone.
- Encouraging each speaker to look at the person they are directing their comments.
- Using a talk partner to prepare ideas before contributing.
- Asking a student to chair the discussion.
- Giving your own opinion and playing devil's advocate.

(adapted from Fisher 2001)

Learning with discussion

Discussion is an effective way of encouraging both critical and creative thinking. By working through ideas as a group, students are encouraged to question their points of view and work out new ideas.

Examining assumptions

Examining assumptions leads people to question their views. Many adults find this difficult because their assumptions have become second nature and part of their commonsense way of looking at the world (Brookfield 1987). Despite young people having spent less time building their assumptions, it can still be a sensitive process. A teacher needs to develop a sense of trust if they are to help students question the basis of their views.

According to Daloz (1986) teachers should:

'toss little bits of disturbing information in their students' paths, little facts and observations, theories and interpretations – cow plops on the road to truth – that raise questions about the students' current world views and invite them to entertain alternatives, to think afresh.'

Critical questioning

Critical questioning aims to encourage reflective thought rather than eliciting information. It is therefore a useful strategy for helping students to question their assumptions. Students may have built what appears to them to be a rational justification for their views. The teacher, who can identify the flaw in reasoning and can pose a question that highlights it and makes the student reflect, has a powerful strategy for developing a critical approach to ideas.

Questions should be specific rather than abstract. In a discussion about government spending decisions, students might have expressed the view that all tax is bad and levels should be cut. A question that asks whether they expect health care to be available for all raises a question about their views. If the response is that they have insurance, a follow-up which asks about a family that hasn't enough money to pay for insurance questions the assumptions again. By working from the specific to the general, students see ideas at work and can then make the transfer to the abstract relationship between taxation and government spending. It is also important to use a non-threatening tone so that students do not feel uncomfortable in being challenged and therefore withdraw. It may take more than one encounter before a student internalises these ideas but the process of questioning such assumptions can help students to consider ideas of fairness and equity.

Students often expect and teachers often ask questions that have only one answer so responses are right or wrong. These are closed questions. Critical questioning means asking open questions that probably have more than one answer and develop higher order skills. The way a question is posed can also influence the answer to the extent that a open question can become closed because the students know that the teacher has only one answer in his or her head.

Critical questioning may start as the domain of the teacher but, as students' experiences of Citizenship develop, such questioning will also be used by the students themselves. Once they start to think about the assumptions being made by others, they are developing a critical, reflective approach to people's perspectives.

At both Key Stages 3 and 4, the Citizenship Programme of Study asks students to 'think about topical political, spiritual, moral, social and cultural issues, problems and events by analysing information and its sources'.

Developing such skills of critical questioning in discussion leads young people to be able to analyse their own perspectives and those of others. These encounters may be with their peers in the classroom, people on the television or written resources.

As discussion often involves groups, critical questioning by teachers or peers leads students to develop their critical thinking skills because they have to rework their ideas in the light of being challenged.

Creative thinking

Creative thinking and Citizenship

Citizenship is not only about what is but also about what might be. Can we imagine a better, fairer and more successful society? What would that be like? How might it be created? We can make a better world and a better society. The question is, 'Where do we begin?'   (Fisher 2003)

Creative thinking is also a key to effective discussion and the development of Citizenship skills and understanding. At Key Stage 3, the Citizenship Programme of Study asks students to 'use their imagination to consider other people's experiences and be able to think about, express and explain views that are not their own'.

At Key Stage 4, they are also asked to critically evaluate views that are not their own. This clearly combines the need for both creative and critical thinking.

Creative thinking can help students to think 'out of the box' and bring alternative solutions to problems. Many of the questions posed in Citizenship benefit from this approach. Critical and creative thinking work hand in hand to develop solutions to such problems because the search is for a better solution. A new solution needs creative thinking. A better solution means that critical approaches must be used as well.

Working creatively is not just the domain of high attainers. In fact students who are successful in formal assessment may be very good at remembering things but there may be little correlation with creativity.

Teaching for creativity should be present throughout the curriculum. It is not just at home in arts subjects. If scientists and entrepreneurs did not work creatively we would be living in a very different world. Wherever there are problems to be solved, a creative approach adds an exciting dimension to the outcomes. In Citizenship this can be achieved through a range of strategies.

Brainstorming

Brainstorming sessions often focus on the solution to a clearly defined problem and form a good beginning for discussion. They should be short and uninhibited and lead to an analysis and evaluation of the ideas. Any idea can be written down in the initial phase because, however ludicrous it sounds, it may contain a kernel of creative wisdom.

Exploring alternative futures

Exploring alternative futures means looking for different ways forward. Many people see the world as a given, something that cannot be changed. Young people are particularly prone to see the world in this way because at home and at school they are under someone else's direction. Developing the ability to speculate on different scenarios for yourself and the community allows students in Citizenship to remove themselves from these constraints. Discussion that focuses on inventing and realising alternative futures is a powerful form of civic education according to Zeigler et al. (1978). The case study in Chapter 5 asks students to work in this way. It is a large-scale activity that asks young people about changing their local community in a particular way. It is a starting point for looking at more fundamental changes that people might like to see.

Achieving creative thinking involves certain types of behaviour from teachers who are often concerned with the search for the 'right' answer. Creative thinking has no right answers in its early stages. All ideas contribute to the pool and some will be selected for development. Teachers and students therefore need to respect the ideas of others in order to free members of the group to contribute their ideas. There is nothing more potent than the sense of ridicule to deter students from joining in.

Figure 3.2

Students need to develop respect for each other if they are to feel confident. The teacher's attitude is crucial to this because it sets the tone and determines the nature of interaction. The first rule of any brainstorm is that people don't laugh at other people's ideas. This immediately gives a sense of security to potential contributors. Treating each other with respect not only facilitates creative thinking but also develops Citizenship understanding and skills.

Case study: Citizenship in KS3 Mathematics

The school

Tunbridge Wells Grammar School for Boys is a large school in an urban environment in Kent. It has 1,100 boys who come from a wide catchment area around the town.

The school runs Citizenship through a mix of discrete lessons, cross-curricular work and extra-curricular activities including a school council. Each department has devised one module, at least one lesson long, that deals with an aspect of Citizenship and fits into its KS3 scheme of work. It can take place in Years 7, 8 or 9. The work is then gathered and assessed by the subject teacher.

The module	Commentary
The Mathematics department devised a module for Year 7 which combines data handling with the development of knowledge of the UK population, its age and gender structure, ethnicity and religious affiliations. It lasts for four to five lessons and intervening homework time.	

Lesson 1

At the beginning of the first lesson, the teacher introduced the activity and explained the role of Citizenship within this section of work.

The class was divided into groups of four and they carried out an introductory activity that set the scene for the rest of the module. The activity involved deciding on the best type of graph to use for each	The activity established the practice they would use for the rest of the module. Each group worked together and discussed the data sets.

short data set and answering a series of questions interpreting the data and its uses. When the work was completed, the class as a whole then discussed the results.

They drew the graph and considered which method was best. The data was shorter and more specific than that used in the main body of the work.

Lessons 2 and 3

The class worked in groups again. Each student was given a set of data. They were asked to prepare a poster containing graphs showing the nature of the UK population. Each graph should have a commentary beside it explaining what it showed and who might find the data useful.

They were asked to work together to decide how the tasks should be organised for this and the next lesson as well as the intervening homework session.

As questions came up, the lesson paused for an impromptu discussion.

The groups allocated the work in a variety of ways. Some selected a complete topic from the data and others worked on one topic and then moved to the next. Each group discussed the text that should accompany each graph in order to work out the implications and people's interest in it.

A student noticed the fact that only 29 per cent of people belonged to the Church of England and asked why it played such a big role in government. Discussion raised issues about whether it should and what might happen in future.

Lesson 4

In the last lesson the students prepared their work for presentation. Posters were created which showed both the graphs and the commentary.

Each group presented their poster and explained the comments they had made. The class as a whole discussed the issues that arose.

The groups generally chose an appropriate graphing method for each data set. Some had looked in detail at each data set, while others had taken a more general approach. This resulted in some groups showing the big picture which others showed patterns within ethnic groupings.

Introductory activity

Citizenship and Mathematics

Data can be displayed in tables and in graphs. There are many statistical graphs and we have to decide which type displays the information best. In this exercise you will have the opportunity to use a number of ways. You need to comment on your findings.

1 This table shows the rate per thousand of population of male and female offenders.

Year	1900	1925	1950	1975	2000
Male	2.0	1.3	5.5	20.8	19.6
Female	0.5	0.1	0.8	4.0	4.1

(a) Use two methods to display this information. Which method do you think shows the trends better? Give a reason.
(b) What do the graphs tell you about criminal offenders?

2 These figures show the number of pupils by school type.

Type of school	Thousands
State nursery	137
State primary	5,345
State secondary	3,886
Non-maintained schools	616
Special schools	114
All schools	10,100

(a) Work out the angles for each sector. Do the angles add up to 360°? Why not?
(b) Draw a pie chart for this data.
(c) Who might be interested in this information?

3 This table shows the percentage of children immunised against measles, mumps and rubella (MMR) and whooping cough by their second birthday.

Year of second birthday	'89	'90	'91	'92	'93	'94	'95	'96	'97	'98	'99
Percentage MMR	80	84	87	90	92	91	91	92	92	91	88
Percentage whooping cough	75	79	84	88	92	93	93	94	94	94	94

(a) Draw a line graph to show this information.
(b) Who might be interested in seeing the trends in immunisation?

4   This table shows the number of females of different ages (thousands)

Age	0–	5–	10–	15–	20–	25–	30–	35–	40–	45–	50–	55–	60–	65–	70–	75–	80–
Wales	91	88	84	105	113	109	89	94	97	80	77	78	83	84	68	60	42
Northern Ireland	67	65	62	67	64	60	53	48	48	42	39	38	37	36	29	25	16

(a) Draw a frequency diagram for the ages in (i) Wales; (ii) Northern Ireland.
(b) Regroup the data into class intervals 0–, 10–, 20–, . . .
(c) Draw two more frequency diagrams with these new intervals.
(d) Which set of class intervals do you think is most useful?
(e) What do your graphs tell you about the ages of females in Wales and Northern Ireland?

Source: Tipler and Vickers 2002

The activity gave the students the opportunity to consider data in a different light. Not only were they being asked to work out the best way to graph data but they also had to consider what it meant and why it might be useful. This activity provided practice for the main activity of the module. It drew on small sets of data so they could be graphed quickly and it provided ideas for the sorts of things to be considered when students were given a freer hand on more complex data.

How did students use the data?

Population size for the United Kingdom is shown in Table 3.1. Different data sets were graphed by different students. Some chose to draw pie charts of the whole population, while others the minority ethnic population (Figures 3.3 and 3.4).

Table 3.1 UK Population 2001

	Total population		Minority ethnic population
	(count)	*(%)*	*(%)*
White	54,153,898	92.1	n/a
Mixed	677,117	1.2	14.6
Asian or Asian British			
Indian	1,053,411	1.8	22.7
Pakistani	747,285	1.3	16.1
Bangladeshi	283,063	0.5	6.1
Other Asian	247,664	0.4	5.3
Black or Black British			
Black Caribbean	565,876	1.0	12.2
Black African	485,277	0.8	10.5
Black Other	97,585	0.2	2.1
Chinese	247,403	0.4	5.3
Other	230,615	0.4	5.0
All minority ethnic population	4,635,296	7.9	*100*
All population	58,789,194	100	n/a

Source: Office for National Statistics 2001.

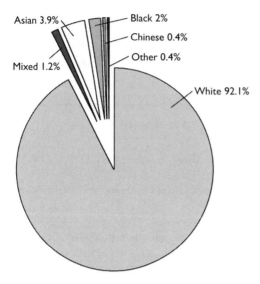

Figure 3.3 UK ethic grouping
Source: Office for National Statistics, 2001.

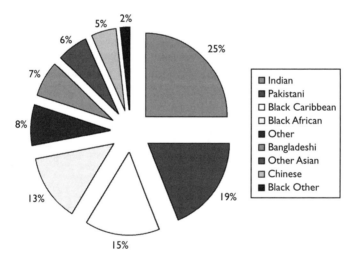

Figure 3.4 The minority ethnic groups
Source: Office for National Statistics, 2001.

The other data included age and gender distribution and projections to 2001, social class distribution and the changing pattern of active faith membership. Discussion revolved around age distribution and led to a realisation that the population was ageing and that this would have implications for the United Kingdom as a whole.

The lesson took place at a time when the role of bishops was in the news. One boy noticed that only 29 per cent of the UK population are practising members of the Church of England. He asked about the role of the church in government and a whole class discussion ensued on the topic.

Any surprises?

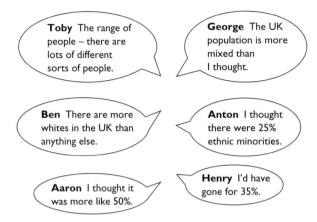

Toby The range of people – there are lots of different sorts of people.

George The UK population is more mixed than I thought.

Ben There are more whites in the UK than anything else.

Anton I thought there were 25% ethnic minorities.

Aaron I thought it was more like 50%.

Henry I'd have gone for 35%.

Figure 3.5

When asked to discuss what surprised them in the data, there was common agreement that the extent and size of the ethnic minority population was different from their expectations.

The students generally agreed that their perceptions of the shape of the UK population came from TV, newspapers, walking round London and football teams.

This section of the activity has strong resonance in the Citizenship context. Many UK citizens have little sense of the actual breakdown of the population in terms of ethnicity. Seeing the evidence clearly came as a surprise to the students and had a significant impact on their thinking.

George TV is always talking about immigrants but there aren't as many as I thought.

It also raises issues for the aspects of the programme of study dealing with the media. George's comment on television and its representation of the immigrant issue provides an insight in how perceptions are developed.

Why gather data?

Jamie If there are loads of children, we'll need more schools.

Toby Loads of old people means more hospitals.

Jamie You need to know where they are so you can build in the right places.

Figure 3.6

Students are often asked to work with data but are not often asked its purpose. In this exercise, they had to consider who might use the data and why. This is an effective way of asking about some of the social issues of relevance to Citizenship.

Alex The government needs to know how many old people's homes to build.

Much of their discussion focused on the way government might use the data. As they worked their way through the different data sets they saw the implications of the changing patterns. The activity not only helped them to develop a picture of the UK population, but also gave them a sense of the reality behind the data. The numbers on the graphs had a greater sense of meaning (Figure 3.6).

Why discuss in groups?

The students clearly relished working in a group. The opportunity to discuss their work both formally and informally enhanced the experience for them.

> **Calham** If you get stuck, you can discuss it with other people and they can help.

> **Ben** You can share ideas.

> **George** It's easier when you have other people to discuss things with.

Some of them found the data quite hard to work with despite being carefully selected. Having the opportunity to share and discuss ideas meant that many students developed a better understanding of the material. This was particularly clear when they explored the uses for the data and who would be interested in it. As this was not an aspect of the data that would normally be considered in the lesson, they had to work together and help each other in order to draw conclusions.

The process enhanced their understanding of the data handling because they had to think about the meaning of the data itself in order to graph it effectively. Because they were more closely engaged with the data, this relationship became clearer.

Discussing in groups and as a whole class also contributed to the development of Citizenship knowledge and understanding. Their analysis of the data was developing an understanding of political, spiritual, social and cultural issues.

Reflection

> **Henry** I could draw graphs and didn't know anything about the UK population.

The activity clearly altered perceptions about the structure of the UK population. All students claimed to know little about it before the series of lessons but discussion showed that they had preconceptions based on the media and other influences. By discussing, graphing and commenting on the data, the module altered misconceptions and painted a much clearer picture for them.

Giving them a free hand to plan and organise the work has great strengths because it gives students practice in prioritising. It does not, however, guarantee every student encountering the key messages of the data. One group for example devoted a lot of time to graphing the age profile for each ethnic minority group but did not see the big picture of the proportionate size of each group in the United Kingdom. In this context, it did not matter because every group produced a poster that, together, did paint the big picture.

The activity would also lend itself to developing ICT skills. Drawing graphs by hand is quite a laborious activity and once mastered can be more quickly and efficiently carried out using a data handling package. The teacher felt she might develop this aspect with future groups. The module could therefore easily be used in an ICT lesson with the focus on developing skills with data-handling packages.

Developing Citizenship understanding and skills

The activity met the needs of Citizenship very effectively. It combined hard facts about the size and shape of the population with the opportunity to share and discuss ideas. In a cross-curricular context, the hard facts can be difficult to integrate so this is a powerful opportunity to use and interpret data.

The key part of the Citizenship Programme of Study that the module covers is 'the diversity of national, regional, religious and ethnic identities in the United Kingdom and the need for mutual respect and understanding'.

The misconceptions that the activity uncovered demonstrate how young people's views can be based on inaccurate information. Correcting this can help to change perspectives. When using data in this way, it is clearly necessary to question students about their interpretations. Many young people look at such information and accept it without comparing it with their own preconceptions. In order to ensure that this is a Citizenship lesson, it is therefore necessary to build in such discussion opportunities.

The nature of the discussion is likely to include aspects such as the media and may also provide an encounter with central government spending when students discuss the uses of the data.

Discussion in both groups and as a class helps young people to develop some of the skills required for Citizenship. Their enjoyment of the experience enhanced learning as they discovered that learning co-operatively had great advantages. All the students felt that they benefited from working together because they shared ideas and supported each other.

The activity would fit into other areas of the curriculum including discrete Citizenship lessons. The focus might shift from creating graphs to the information within the data but the format could be maintained.

Discussion across the curriculum

Business Studies

Should a business use controversial material to market its product? Examples of such advertising provide a good stimulus.

Design and Technology

How does the product meet people's different needs and likes? The PIES approach that looks at physical, intellectual, emotional and social (PIES) needs is a useful way of asking students to consider the issue.

English

What makes an effective deterrent for a young criminal? This might be accompanied by examples of how young people have been dealt with in a range of books.

Geography

Which site should be chosen for the dam? This can be based on a simulated or real example.

History

What makes a good leader? This discussion topic is used widely in KS3. The comparison of the effect of different leaders makes a good start. Students should consider the impact such leadership styles would have today.

ICT

Once students have gathered information on any Citizenship topic, group discussion can be used to select information to create a poster or leaflet. The group should include the rationale for selection as a commentary with the product.

Modern Foreign Languages (MFL)

How do festivals in . . . compare with those in the United Kingdom?

Music

What choice of music would best represent our school community?

Religions Education (RE)

Group discussion on any moral issue such as 'Is it wrong to steal?' stimulates contributions. Following group discussion with written or oral feedback often works better than whole-class discussion.

Science

What might happen if too many parents decided not to have their children vaccinated? Use the activity sheet http://www.sycd.co.uk/can_we_should_we/pdf/immunisation/im_whatif.pdf together with related teaching notes at http://www.sycd.co.uk/can_we_should_we/pdf/immunisation/im_teach.pdf

Questions for reflection

- Identify discussion topics in your subject that develop Citizenship understanding.
- What subject knowledge and skills are you trying to develop?
- What Citizenship knowledge and skills are being developed?
- How will you measure achievement in both subject areas?
- What evidence do you have of student achievement? Compare your evidence with evidence from other teachers in your department and from other subjects. Are there ideas that you and your colleagues might use to improve the quality of your work?

Chapter 4

Thinking through debate

Why debate?

Debate is part of any democratic process. It also underpins the development of reasoned argument and an appreciation of other people's points of view. In developing skills of inquiry and communication, the Citizenship programme of study expects students at Key Stages 3 and 4 to 'take part in debates'. By KS4 these should be formal so opportunities should be found within the curriculum to work with a chairperson, speakers for the proposition, speakers for the opposition and an audience vote. Debate is a structured process which requires students to listen to arguments, contribute and question before making a decision about their own point of view.

Many young people are strong proponents of one point of view and are unwilling to listen to others. Creating a formal environment provides a structure in which they can develop skills which help them to appreciate that other people may have valid ideas. The formality itself can be helpful in the classroom because it provides a structure for a lesson and gives both evidence and arguments to support a point of view.

To contribute to a debate, students have to 'research a topical political, spiritual, moral, social or culture issue, problem or event by analysing information from different sources' as the programme of study requires.

To evaluate the outcome of a debate, students have to be able to weigh up opposing points of view and come to their own conclusions. This meets the Programme of Study's requirement to 'express, justify and defend orally and in writing a personal opinion about such issues, problems or events'.

Using debate

Debate can be used in the classroom in a variety of ways. Within a lesson, it can be used to sum up a topic and show a democratic decision. It could also be used in an almost impromptu way if students are demonstrating strong divergence of opinion as it makes them think hard about the arguments on each side.

The formal process of debate involves at least five people and an audience.

The chair

The chair can be either the teacher or a member of the class. This role is important in both guiding the debate and managing the process. On the first occasion, it is therefore wise for the teacher to take the chair in order to demonstrate how a debate runs and ensure that the speakers get a hearing. Once the practice is established, students can take over the role as this develops Citizenship skills. The chair has to take responsibility for ensuring that everyone shows respect for people who hold different opinions.

Issue for debate

The issue for debate is best based on values or policy. Fact is not a successful focus because it can leave little for debate once the details are known. It is difficult to argue against clear evidence although a discussion on the difference between fact and value judgement can be useful. Once upon a time, a debate on whether the world is flat or round might have been interesting but facts now tell us the answer. It might produce some entertaining contributions from students with a great sense of humour but adds little to their understanding of Citizenship.

Debating a value involves looking at what is right and wrong. Because people have different perspectives, right and wrong may not be clear cut. A topic like animal rights stirs the emotions of many students and their point of view will depend on their perspectives on the relationship between animals and people.

A policy can be at any level from the school, the local community, national or global. Should students wear uniform? Should the local council build a skate park? Should 16 and 17 year olds be allowed to vote? Should the European Union and the United States cut subsidies to farmers to help less economically developed countries?

Policies and values provide a better basis for debate because there is more scope for different perspectives. If there is clear evidence that facts are facts, there is little scope for discussion. People can hold different views on values and policies so there is more scope for debate.

Speakers for and against

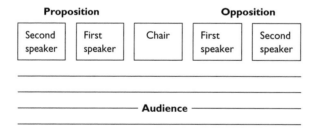

Figure 4.1 The structure of debate

The speakers for and against the proposition will be drawn from the class. The nature of the debate will be different if students fervently support or oppose the topic of the debate. If they are committed to a particular point of view, they will generally debate with more enthusiasm but may be less willing to listen to others or consider changing their minds. If an issue has less personal support or antipathy, the balance of argument may be more critical.

Students can also learn from being asked to take a stand point which is contrary to the personal opinion. It makes them think hard about the logic of the point of view as well as challenging their own attitude.

Speeches

The speeches should be time limited. The length of time will depend on the students' age and their research opportunities. A quick debate which asks students to draw their reasoning together might just give two minutes per person. A topic that has had more research time will need five minutes per speaker. The first speaker for the proposition has his or her say initially, followed by the first speaker for the opposition. The second speakers then have their turn.

Questioning of speakers

Questioning of speakers can happen at various points in the debate but the ground rules need to be set out clearly at the beginning. The structure will depend on the time available and the nature of the debate.

In a formal debate, opposition speakers can ask for 'a point of information' at any time. Their request may be turned down by the speaker with a sweep of the hand! This can be hard to manage and is probably better not used in the initial stages of developing debating skills.

The opposition speakers and the audience, depending on time, should be allowed to question after each speech. If time is short, audience questions might be asked when all speakers have made their contributions.

As questioning is an integral part of debate, speakers must identify questions they think they might be asked if they are to be able to defend their point of view effectively. Students should also be encouraged to think of likely questions to ask speakers while carrying out their research.

The whole process helps to develop critical thinking and apply it in the context of Citizenship issues.

Involving the whole class

Involving the whole class is important because most students learn little from simply listening and short attention spans can lead to disruption. It is therefore a good idea to build debate into a series of lessons which require everyone to contribute.

Preparation during the previous lesson will include everyone. Ideas can be gathered from the class so that the arguments for and against are beginning to be assembled. An interactive white board can be helpful because all the ideas can be gathered together, sorted, printed and handed out to the class. Students can be helped to sort arguments if they are presented on cards. A matching and sorting task in pairs or small groups helps to identify similar and different viewpoints.

Having developed a structure for the argument, students can then research the issue according to their role. Speakers may represent a group rather than just themselves so research must be pooled and the speech developed together. Some members of a group might be asked to work on the questions to challenge the opposition.

Quick debates often mean limited research time unless internet-connected computers are available. They do, however, encourage students to structure their thinking and be prepared for their ideas to be challenged.

Preparing the speeches

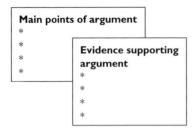

Preparing the speeches in a group keeps everyone involved. A brainstorm of ideas needs to be turned into a sequenced argument. Setting out the point with plenty of space to develop each point provides the essence of the speech. A writing frame can be used to help to structure thinking. The group can then work on each point in pairs or individually so that everyone has made a contribution.

Figure 4.2

Voting

Voting takes place at the end of the debate and the proposition is carried or defeated. It is interesting to discover whether people have changed their minds in the course of the event. A quick vote at the beginning will provide the evidence.

Learning through debate

Critical thinking

Debate requires students to:

- work out a logical argument to support their case
- listen carefully to other people and devise questions that challenge their argument.

Both these activities help the development of critical thinking, a key contributor to the development of Citizenship skills and understanding.

Young people are presented with a wide range of views and opinions on many issues but are most often influenced by their families and peer groups. Their attitudes may therefore be ones that they have accepted as the norm without giving them much consideration.

The Citizenship Programme of Study expects students at Key Stage 3 to understand 'the diversity of national, regional, religious and ethnic identities in the United Kingdom and the need for mutual respect and understanding'.

The ability to build a reasoned argument to support your point of view and question others plays a significant role in the development of such understanding. As students work in this way, they are developing the skills necessary for critical thinking.

Critical thinking is described by Fisher (2001) as:

- learning how to question, when to question and what questions to ask
- learning how to reason, when to use reasoning and what reasoning methods to use.

These have been exemplified as a set of questions by several people but the questions that seem most useful in this context were developed by Robert Ennis (1962) because they involve a set of statements and related questions which can be applied to both evidence that students are using in research and their own contributions to debate.

Encouraging students to work with the questions gives them a framework to build their own reasoned arguments and to evaluate those of others.

Criterion	Question
Grasping the meaning of a statement.	Is it meaningful?
Judging whether there is an ambiguity in reasoning.	Is it clear?
Judging whether statements contradict each other.	Is it consistent?
Judging whether conclusions follow necessarily.	Is it logical?
Judging whether a statement is specific enough.	Is it precise?
Judging whether a statement applies a principle.	Is it following a rule?
Judging whether an observation statement is reliable.	Is it accurate?
Judging whether an inductive conclusion is warranted.	Is it justified?
Judging whether the problem has been identified.	Is it relevant?
Judging whether something is an assumption.	Is it taken for granted?
Judging whether a definition is adequate.	Is it well defined?
Judging whether a statement taken on authority is acceptable.	Is it true?

Whether developing the case for or against the proposition in a debate or being part of the audience and casting a vote, students need to use knowledge and the skills of comprehension, application, analysis, synthesis and evaluation (Bloom 1956). This process is essential to developing an argument or casting a vote. Voting means listening to two opposing sets of arguments, evaluating and judging them against your criteria.

A change of views shows clearly when a vote is taken before the debate as well as at the end. The plenary session can identify the reasons for any changes.

Fair-minded thinking

In Citizenship, the aim is to develop 'fair-minded thinkers' (Paul *et al.* 1986) as opposed to 'selfish thinkers' or 'uncritical thinkers'. Selfish thinkers have the skills required to organise arguments but do so from an egocentric point of view and set out to manipulate other people. Uncritical thinkers are vulnerable because they have weak skills and can easily be manipulated. The audience in a debate should be developing the skills required to become fair-minded thinkers.

There are two important skills which influence the achievement of fair-minded thinking.

- Understanding differences leads students to develop an appreciation of other people's perspectives. Unless a student can understand that other people have different points of view, it is difficult for them to develop a fair-minded approach.
- Evaluating the processes involved in building an argument and coming to conclusions. This might involve working out the purpose of rules, activities or decisions rather than just accepting them as given. Students are therefore developing criteria to evaluate the outcomes.

The combination of these two skills enables students to look at an issue and work out their standpoint and explain it. The criteria are critical because if different members of a class are using different criteria, their conclusions are likely to be different. It may therefore be necessary to agree a list of criteria for everyone to use.

Fair-minded thinking in practice . . .

Cigarettes should be banned!

In any class of 11 to 16 year olds, there are likely to be some smokers who are prepared to defend the right to smoke. If the argument is unstructured, however, it might become a debate with little purpose and even less learning.

A debate about banning cigarettes will involve some research into the laws themselves, the reasons for the laws and the effect of smoking. Equally questions might be raised on freedom of choice and the impact of a ban.

The students might be asked to consider their criteria before the debate in order to give themselves some yardsticks for assessing the arguments. In the early stages of learning about debate, this might be done formally as part of the teaching. As students gain experience, they will recognise the importance of establishing clear criteria and will need less support and prompting to do so.

Possible criteria include the following:

- impact on individual's health
- impact on other people
- cost to society of illness
- the importance of freedom to do something
- the importance of freedom from other people's actions
- what makes a law good or bad?

Students would then need to be able to balance these factors in order to decide how to cast their votes.

Arguing but not quarrelling

The structure of debate provides opportunities to learn to argue but not to quarrel. When people hold very different points of view on a topic, it can be difficult to persuade them to listen to each other and evaluate the points of view. If a group is made up of uncritical thinkers and egocentric thinkers, the outcomes are predictable. They may be equally predictable if groups are based on friendships because people are often attracted to others who are of the same mindset.

Debate, whether formal or informal, asks students to deal with an issue within a framework. It therefore provides a structure which facilitates listening and evaluating while dissuading people from attacking each other because of their differences. This chapter's case study illustrates one teacher's strategy for teaching rules to students with little experience of debates. By allocating points for different types of contributions, the students are encouraged to demonstrate logical argument and participation in the debate. This encourages arguing and discourages quarrelling.

Case study: Citizenship in KS3 History

The school

Lacon Childe is an 11–16 school in Cleobury Mortimer, Shropshire. The Citizenship co-ordinator is also Head of History. A school audit led to development work across KS3 in History, Geography, English and Science with some support work such as 'the nature of democracy' unit taught within a PHSE timetable.

In Year 9 History, for example, students study the Holocaust from a variety of perspectives and consider the implications for today's society. English lessons look at the ways in which events are reported in today's media and how bias can be detected in verbal and written reports.

The school also encourages active participation through a series of awards for personal, craft, physical and community challenges. Year 10 students, for example, regularly run Christmas parties for local senior citizens.

The lesson	Commentary
Aims	
• To review key ideas from previous lessons on the Industrial Revolution. • To identify its impact on the lives of the UK population using terms such as freedom. • To develop skills of argument and counter-argument.	This lesson is used as a good summary exercise following the teaching of a KS3 History unit. Students are asked to identify causes and consequences and to use supporting data. The skills of debate are to be built up over several lessons and will contribute to students' citizenship skills as well as improve their participation in history lessons.
Background and content	
A Year 8 class has two 50-minute lessons of history each week. They have spent four weeks looking at various aspects of the industrial revolution using textbooks, discussions and investigative work in pairs and in small groups.	The links between industrial developments and the quality of life of the community, employers and workers has a resonance with today's politics. Students are encouraged to use ideas such as freedom to inform their judgements.
The starter	
Some prompt questions are used to recap the key developments of the Industrial Revolution. Students are asked if the changes from 1700 to 1900 made people free. Individuals were asked	The teacher helps students to identify an important criterion which can be used to assess the consequences of change. He challenges students to interpret the meaning of 'freedom' and draws together whole class ideas. He has used freedom

to explain what it meant to be free. An overhead projector (OHP) slide was used to summarise the main ideas. (10 minutes)

and other criteria in planning the next stage of the lesson.

The core

Students work in small groups on a bank of resource materials. They sort out items which offer evidence of a group of people being made more or less free by changes in the industrial environment. Each student writes a summary of the group findings using a writing frame. (10 minutes)

The class is then divided into two with one half to argue the case 'for' and one against the notion of more freedom. The key rules for debate are outlined using the board.

The two groups have a few moments to prepare, chairs are rearranged so that the groups face each other. The teacher keeps a tally of points awarded for good ideas and for good 'counter-arguments'. (20 minutes)

Students have seen most of the source materials before but in different contexts such as an extract from a textbook.

The variety of materials includes interview and speech extracts, as well as pictures. Some sources are contradictory, some complementary, and some from different time periods. This range is intended to provide students with ideas for their statements and arguments; the material is of varying difficulty.

Debating rules limit contributions from each student so this prevents domination by the articulate few. Extra points for counter-argument encourage listening skills and logical thinking. The three points awarded to the team with most participants proved decisive in determining the 'winning team'.

Students were asked for their views about what makes for a good debate at the start and end of the activity.

Plenary

A brief review involved the teacher putting questions to named individuals. (10 minutes)

Some answers showed a good grasp of the idea of freedom applied to living in better housing conditions, to escape from slavery, to an opportunity for better jobs. A few students suggested that the evidence could run both ways.

Some appeared ready to change their original view about the consequences of the industrial revolution as a result of the debate.

Some students made an oral contribution in front of the whole class for the first time. It was clear to the class that the more people taking part in the debate meant 'more points'!

The debate was followed up with a written task requiring an in-depth explanation of the meaning of freedom and the impact of the Industrial Revolution in the United Kingdom and abroad.

Students had been asked to express their personal views of freedom and to take account of others' views in examining evidence from another time period. They had to sort, prioritise and provide verbal summaries of historical events. Some succeeded in making statements: a few recognised evidence that ran counter to an opposition view. A very few identified a modern source of evidence which implied there is still a way to go before everyone has freedom even today. The implications of this for thinking critically about today's society are important.

Will every student recognise this as good citizenship?

Will students transfer these skills of debate to a new history context, with and then without the support of source materials?

Will students use these debating rules for themselves in other subjects or outside school?

The starter

Did the industrial revolution make people free?
In your pair decide on your own definition of what freedom is.
Freedom is ....
....

Our pair believe that the industrial revolution *did/did not* make people more free.
Our five most important pieces of evidence to support this view are:
*
*
*

Figure 4.3

The discussion

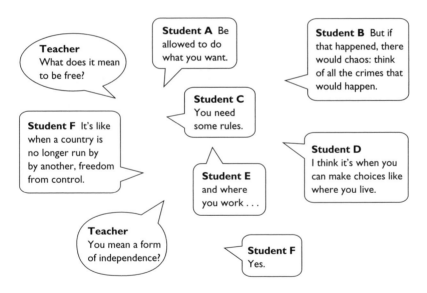

Figure 4.4

Preparing for the debate

Your pair will be told whether you agree or disagree with the statement that:

'The Industrial Revolution made people more free'

Each pair must note down five points that support your viewpoint. Use the resources to work out what you think. You should choose ideas that you think are most important and that you can explain clearly. You will only have a few minutes to do this so you cannot write in detail.

A sample of the evidence used in the debate

From the eighteenth century onwards more people campaigned for the abolition of slavery. One working-class white British man said in 1794:

'Slavery is insulting to human nature. Its abolition will promote the cause of liberty. It will avenge peacefully ages of wrongs to our negro brothers.'

New trade made demands for British goods. This meant more jobs for British workers. Many people benefited from these new jobs as it gave them a regular wage and new opportunities in the towns.

Jonathan Downe – a child who worked in a cotton factory – was interviewed by Parliament on 6 June 1832.

Figure 4.5

'When I was seven years old, I started work at Mr. Marshall's factory at Shrewsbury. If a child was drowsy, the overlooker touches the child on the shoulder and says, "Come here". In a corner of the room there is an iron cistern filled with water. He takes the boy by the legs and dips him in the cistern and sends him back to work.'

First task: sorting and selecting the evidence

Ben and Dan start work.

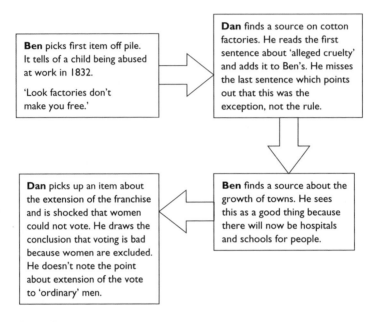

Ben picks first item off pile. It tells of a child being abused at work in 1832.

'Look factories don't make you free.'

Dan finds a source on cotton factories. He reads the first sentence about 'alleged cruelty' and adds it to Ben's. He misses the last sentence which points out that this was the exception, not the rule.

Dan picks up an item about the extension of the franchise and is shocked that women could not vote. He draws the conclusion that voting is bad because women are excluded. He doesn't note the point about extension of the vote to 'ordinary' men.

Ben finds a source about the growth of towns. He sees this as a good thing because there will now be hospitals and schools for people.

Figure 4.6

Second task: the debate

Rules of the debate

- Each person may speak a maximum of three times.
- Everyone must listen in silence to each person's ideas.
- For each valid point made your team will receive one mark.
- For each valid challenge to a point made by the opposing team the mark will be transferred to the opposing team.
- No valid points receive no marks.
- The team with the most participants receives an additional bonus of three points.

Hint: the clearer, more thoughtful and detailed points will be more
difficult for the opposing team to challenge.

The teams debate

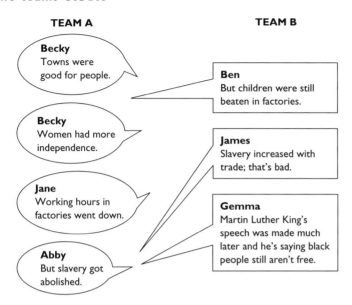

Figure 4.7

Reflection

The lesson aimed to develop Citizenship ideas and skills of critical thinking through discussion and debate in history. This involved developing understanding and a proactive attitude to freedom through understanding the past.

Understanding the past

* Arriving at a personal opinion of what freedom is/might be.
* Developing an understanding of how people can have different interpretations of the same idea.
* Using contemporary and non-contemporary sources to build different views of the past.
* Encouraging active participation in discussion and debate.
* Developing listening skills.
* Thinking about whether actions or attitudes were more important in shaping people's lives in the eighteenth and nineteenth centuries.

To demonstrate their understanding of these issues, the students produced a piece of writing focusing on the meaning of freedom and whether the changes of the Industrial Revolution led to any real changes in the freedom of people in both the United Kingdom and other countries. They were encouraged to use their discussion as a springboard for developing more complex explanations that do not rely purely on narrative or description but include a measure of analysis using questions such as 'How much?' and 'How important?' They were also encouraged to challenge different interpretations and simplistic ideas by using 'but' and 'however' in their responses.

What the teacher thought

- The students had a real challenge when using sources in the debate.
- Some were using 'today's' view of towns, jobs etc. to judge changes of the past.
- It was difficult to set freedom from slavery alongside freedom to live in decent housing. Which deserves a greater priority?
- Some lines of argument were very superficial. This is bad or good?
- Some extracts were easier to paraphrase than others.
- The points scoring certainly motivated most of the class, though there was a temptation to join in at any cost towards the end.
- The teacher has a tough job to rule on the various contributions in a simple and fair way.
- Would it help students to transfer the debating skills to their own contemporary lives if a debate about modern freedom was part of the follow-on lessons?

Developing Citizenship understanding

History provides many opportunities for developing Citizenship because it involves investigating how people behaved towards each other. The lesson clearly develops the way students think about aspects of the Citizenship Programme of Study including: 'the legal and human rights and responsibilities underpinning society' and 'the need for mutual respect and understanding'.

The stages of the activity allowed students to explore their ideas of freedom today and work with evidence about freedom in the past. In sorting the evidence, the class discovered a range of evidence which showed both sides of the picture. These examples were used to support the debate.

There is also evidence that some students tend to look at historical evidence with modern eyes.

Dan picks up an item about the extension of the franchise and is shocked that women could not vote. He draws the conclusion that voting is bad because women are excluded. He doesn't note the point about extension of the vote to 'ordinary' men.

It is therefore important that teachers help them to make links between past and present contexts if historical experiences are to be translated into Citizenship.

Developing Citizenship skills

The rules set up for the debate clearly encouraged students to participate. Students who had never said anything before joined in on this occasion. It therefore helped members of the class to develop sufficient confidence to contribute.

Although the rule was double edged, in that students started to join in for the sake of it in order to gain points, they were making the first steps to achieve one of the skills included in the Citizenship Programme of Study: 'to contribute to group and exploratory class discussions, and take part in debates.'

As debate was a new experience for this class, they found it hard to abide by the rules. As they become more confident the rules can be applied more rigorously.

The class found preparing for their first debate a challenging activity. Having to work with the resource material, select from it and put it to work to support their argument was demanding. It again provided them with a springboard to start to meet the requirements of the Programme of Study which asks students to: 'think about topical political, spiritual, moral, social and cultural issues, problems and events by analysing information and its sources'.

> **Dan** finds a source on cotton factories. He reads the first sentence about 'alleged cruelty' and adds it to Ben's. He misses the last sentence which points out that this was the exception, not the rule.

In this early stage of skill development, it is interesting to see how some students use evidence to support their point of view and ignore parts which do not.

As students become more practised in working with sources in this way, they should become more discriminating in their use and learn to evaluate the evidence more effectively. Perhaps such techniques of selection help them to understand the significance of media in society as well.

In the debate students were asked to take a stand 'for' or 'against' the motion. They had to carry out their research to support a given perspective. Even if they personally disagreed, they had to produce a reasoned argument for or against the statement. This clearly provides a good opportunity to develop the skills required by the Programme of Study: 'to use their imagination to consider other people's experiences and to be able to think about, express and explain views that are not their own'.

Enhancing Citizenship

The teacher who ran the debate asked the following question: 'Would it help students to transfer the debating skills to their own contemporary lives if a debate about modern freedom was part of the follow-on lessons?'

This highlights an issue that crops up frequently in cross-curricular Citizenship teaching. The students had made considerable strides in the development of Citizenship skills in History. There was, however, a degree of uncertainty about the transfer of ideas from the historical context to the current environment.

It is therefore important to devise an activity that helps students to translate the experience to their own lives. The outcomes of such an activity can then be included in the students' Citizenship Portfolios and therefore provide evidence for KS3 assessment.

Debates across the curriculum

Business Studies

Ethics should always influence business decisions.

English

Debate on any topical issue builds skills in speaking, listening, group discussion and interaction.

Geography

Is free trade fair?

ICT

Debates on a current topic can be run electronically with appropriate software. They might be related to an issue in school or beyond.

MFL

A current topic related to the experiences and perspectives of people in the country or community.

RE

Debate can be based on just about any moral issue such as 'Everyone has the right to hold their own views'.

Science

Is space research a waste of public funds? This activity sheet provides a starting point for debate: http://www.ase.org.uk/htm/teacher_zone/upd8/upd8_13/upd8_13_pdfs/galileo.pdf. Related teaching notes can be found at http://www.ase.org.uk/htm/teacher_zone/upd8/upd8_13/upd8_galileo.php.

Questions for reflection

- What topic in your subject lends itself to a debate, either formal or informal, which will develop citizenship understanding?
- Work out a set of criteria that a class might use to debate a topic of your choice.
- How would you ensure that the students have transferred the ideas to the context of Citizenship?

Chapter 5

Investigating Citizenship

Why investigate?

When students leave school, they need to put into practice the skills and knowledge that they have acquired during Citizenship lessons. Voting, shopping or looking for a job requires investigative skills and the use of knowledge to make sense of very different kinds of information. Investigation in school not only helps students to develop these skills but can also capture their imagination. It has specific advantages in managing information and perspectives, learning and transferring skills and helping students to become independent learners. These aspects are explored by looking at the outcomes of an investigation that schools carried out and the nature of assistance that can be given to non-expert teachers to help them guide students effectively.

Managing information and perspectives

Investigation provides the opportunity to think about issues, to consider appropriate data, and to see how looking at things from different perspectives leads people to come to different conclusions.

An investigation into the quality of school meals, for example, could help students to see that people have different values. The quality may look different if judged by nutritional standards, student tastes or costs, so there may be very different views about the 'ideal caterer'.

Investigation can be seen as a crucial element in helping students to link data and theories or models used to 'explain' the data (Kuhn 1989; Driver et al. 1996). Young students tend to see data and explanations as interchangeable; older students often ignore data which conflict with their own explanations. Investigations can teach students that there may be different explanations, and that different 'models' can be used to explain data in different ways.

Learning and transferring skills

An investigation into the meaning of poverty might ask students to consider what counts as evidence of poverty. They might select and classify data and then decide on the best items to be used for different purposes. 'How much should the government pay in benefits?' or 'How can a charity help the poor?' might need different approaches. As a result they would learn about poverty but also about different ways of classifying data related to poverty. The challenge to 'think about their thinking' is likely to make them more sensitive to their assumptions about poverty and recognise how classification is being used elsewhere.

It is possible to teach students such higher order skills through investigation and there is evidence of both deeper understanding and greater transferability when compared with strategies which simply require students to acquire knowledge (Shayer and Adey 1994).

Becoming independent learners

In investigative work students can be put in a position where they have to make their own decisions about the selection, collection and classification of evidence. They may take part in a group activity where leadership and collaboration are at a premium. This may involve, for example, investigating and reporting back on a particular issue. In such situations, students learn to make their own judgements and to test them out within safe boundaries. With help, they can learn to use appropriate strategies and to evaluate their own progress. Assisting students to develop these procedural skills and autonomy as a learner should therefore be an integral part of any Citizenship course.

Motivating students

Investigative activities can be fun and therefore motivate a wide range of students. Teachers have been surprised to find students pursuing ideas and issues beyond lessons with an unanticipated level of enthusiasm.

There is evidence from interviews which shows how students valued engaging in activities with clear links to the outside world and a focus on current events which caught their interest and were meaningful to them (Wallace 1996).

Case study: KS3 Citizenship investigations in school

The use of investigation as a teaching strategy in Citizenship is explored through *The Campaign*, an activity developed by the Nuffield Foundation and used in several schools across Britain including Rhodesway School in Bradford. The process is analysed, evaluated and used to draw general conclusions about the use of investigation.

The school

Rhodesway School, Bradford, faces a range of challenges. It is a large 11–18 school with over 1,800 students. Bradford's schools have recently been reorganised from a middle-school structure. The school has had to work hard to create a new ethos. It has recently become a specialist arts college.

Many of the students come from disadvantaged backgrounds, which is reflected by the number of students having free school meals. At 41 per cent, this is twice the national average and increasing. The school has a growing proportion of students from ethnic minorities. In five years the intake changed from 60 per cent white and 40 per cent ethnic minorities to 38 per cent white and 62 per cent ethnic minorities; 56 per cent have English as an additional language. Some of these are at a very early stage of language acquisition. Academic attainment on entry is significantly below the national average.

On arrival, students have little experience of working in a multicultural environment because they come from primary schools which are largely or wholly Asian or white. The school is located in an almost wholly white district of Bradford and therefore has few links with the local community.

At the time the school first carried out *The Campaign*, Citizenship was being trialled in tutor groups. There is now a dedicated team who have volunteered or been invited to participate. The subject is allocated one hour per week.

The Campaign

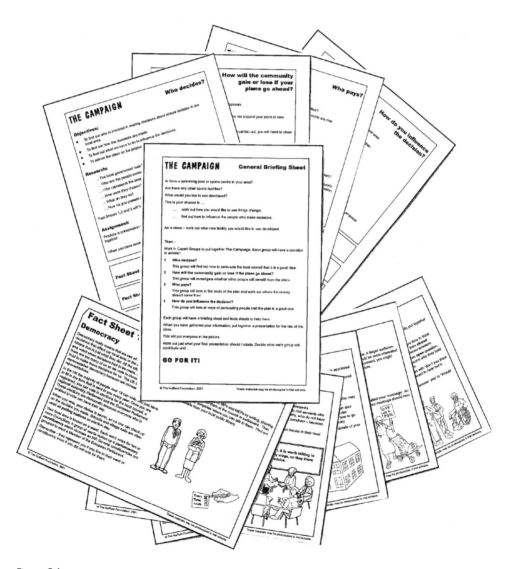

Figure 5.1
Source: Nuffield Foundation website

The *Campaign* is a KS4 investigation which covers aspects of local government, media and community participation as well as many of the skills of enquiry, communication, participation and responsible action. Students are asked to decide on a leisure facility which they would like to see in their community and create a campaign to persuade people to develop it. Final presentations might be made to representatives from the council or other interested outsiders. *The Campaign* takes place over six one-hour lessons but can be adapted to fit different situations. It is copyright free and can be downloaded from the Nuffield Foundation website.

How the investigation works

Lesson 1: Introduction to the investigation

The class discusses the need for leisure facilities in the local area and decides on one or more proposals.

The class then divides into groups which work out how to approach the investigation. There are four 'expert groups' for an investigation.

Organisation

The teacher explains the investigation and the activities involved.

The number of proposals needs to be guided by the size of the class: the investigative work requires good sized groups and students like to suggest proposals of their own: too many proposals might prove challenging to manage.

Lessons 2–3

(Plus homework time if available)
Expert Groups carry out research and prepare a presentation. The presentations aim to help the class as a whole to create the proposal.

The whole class plans the presentation of the chosen proposal. This could involve a variety of strategies. A written report, a leaflet, a website, a press release, a PowerPoint presentation, video or a combination of all of these. The media group will have advised on this.

Allocation of final tasks to groups.

Resources

Students will require access to the briefing sheet, group task sheets and the relevant fact sheets. Copies of Yellow Pages and local phone books provide useful research material. Access to a telephone, fax machine and computers would be useful but not essential. Many local authorities have websites which will help the research process.

Groups may need prompts to help them organise their tasks, to shape their presentation, or reminders to consider other people's viewpoints.

Lessons 4–5

Completion of work on presentation. Rehearsal of presentation.

Given likely time constraints, students will need to be prompted about careful selection of data, on allocation of tasks, ensuring a sense of audience. The availability of ICT resources will be an important factor.

Lesson 6

Final presentation to independent person, if possible.

Questioning of group and discussion about the success of *The Campaign*. What could be improved?

Teacher prompts are important to ensure students evaluate not only the proposal but also their approach to the business of campaigning. Useful questions might include:

1   How do you justify this spending by the council?
2   What would you suggest the council cut back on in order to be able to afford it?
3   What advice would you give to people who wanted to make their voices heard by the local council?
4   What are the advantages of decisions being taken in this way? Are there disadvantages as well?

Outcomes

Rhodesway was one of a group of schools in Britain which used *The Campaign*. The following examples are drawn from the experiences of these schools. The outcomes show how *The Campaign* contributes both to the knowledge and skills included in the Citizenship Programme of Study.

Information and perspectives

Most students knew little of the workings of local democracy nor appreciated the extent to which people had different perspectives before they embarked upon *The Campaign*. Their presentations at both stages of the activity demonstrated that they had effectively gathered and interpreted information that they shared with others.

We'd have to persuade them to spend less on other activities.

> Some of our mates wanted to do something different.

Students who gathered opinions were quickly introduced to the idea of perspectives and demonstrated in their presentations that they appreciated that these views had to be taken into account.

The questions they asked other people also reflected a developing awareness of other perspectives.

> Why do you think we should do it your way?

Learning and transferring skills

Students had plenty of opportunities to develop higher order skills. The use of the questionnaire, for example, meant that they had to transfer the ideas on a fact sheet to generate one in their own context.

> We decided that local radio and the local papers were better than local telly because the telly covered a much bigger area so people wouldn't be so interested.

They were also required to classify and interpret the information they gathered in their fields of investigation. An expert group, which had looked at the local media, evaluated their results effectively.

Becoming independent learners

To help students develop as independent learners, *The Campaign* was differentiated in a variety of ways in different schools. One school simplified the fact sheets for some students. Another broke down the tasks into bite-sized parts for students who had difficulty in dealing with the big picture. This needs to be done carefully if students are not to lose that sense of investigation. Groups were selected with care in order to make the most of individuals' skills and abilities.

Many students acquired new skills and gained confidence in carrying them out. This was enhanced when their efforts resulted in positive outcomes. The students who set up an appointment for a telephone interview with the mayor, not only put their point of view and gathered a wealth of information but also developed an understanding of how to make contact with appropriate people.

> The person we spoke to first suggested we made an appointment. The mayor had time to think about our questions and to talk to us.

In one school the staff were surprised at the outcomes. *The Campaign* had been deemed to be too difficult for their students because they lacked the necessary skills and resources were limited. A very short period had been allocated for the final presentations because teachers felt that the students would have little to say. In the event, much to the surprise of the staff, another time slot had to be provided because of the high quality of the presentations. The students had demonstrated their ability to become independent learners.

Groups of students who were unaccustomed to making presentations, stood up and put their point of view both in class and to a wider audience. Rhodesway School made the presentation a formal event with outsiders forming part of the audience.

Motivation

To whom it may concern

During the week 29th Sept.–2nd Nov. We, as a year, were asked to set up a campaign in our individual form and present it to the year itself, head teacher, members of staffs and cancellers. The campaign has been a widely experience for us towards the outside work, Where we given the chance to have a say in what our town should and shouldn't offer us. It was a discussion exercise were we discussed matters.

The campaign has got me thinking about stuffs, which I would our town to have. It has given me the courage to stand up and firth for it. It has been a very lively week where we all thought about our hometown and what we could do to improve it or what we would like to see there.

I would personally like to thank all the people who provided us with the helpful l sheets, their time and their effort to make our campaign a lot easier. I will still be carrying on my campaign on the snow dome.

Yours faithfully

Nadia

In Nadia's school, *The Campaign* was run during one week. Every class in the year group had a lesson every day. Her letter was unsolicited and demonstrates how students from across the ability range can find investigation motivating.

In one school, an individual teacher had involved the local councillor. She had joined the lesson, listened and discussed the students' plans. The knowledge, understanding and attitude of the students in this class were significantly different from other classes in which teachers were less committed to the subject and the activity.

Local interest is often a motivating factor. In one school, which was bidding to become a sports college, the students were enthused by basing their investigation on the facilities which they felt were most appropriate for this new development.

Developing teachers' skills

After completing *The Campaign*, students were asked if it had changed their percep-tions of the part they could play in changing things (Figure 5.2). Teachers were also asked to fill in a questionnaire. There was a clear relationship between the skills and attitudes of teachers and the response of their students. The following section looks at ways in which the Citizenship team can be helped to encourage investigative skills in their students.

Has the activity affected the way you think about how you can affect things?

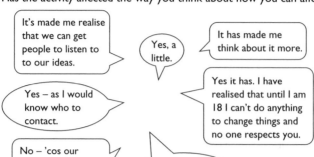

Figure 5.2

Helping students to work with information and perspectives

Matching intentions and perception

There is often a mismatch between the teacher's intentions in a lesson and students' perceptions. Evidence shows that in cases where the teacher meant over 50 per cent of the lesson to be about investigative skills and about 30 per cent to be content-focused, the students' perceptions were a mirror image, with 74 per cent believing the lesson to be mainly about content and only 20 per cent seeing the emphasis on skills (Watson and Wood-Robinson 1998).

To overcome this, it is important that the objectives of investigative lessons are clearly shared. Students must be able to see the 'big picture' so the plan must be clear. Equally, it is important not to jump too far ahead so the plan needs to be revisited frequently. Posting past work on the school's intranet is a good way to meet both these objectives because it can be shared by all and demonstrates what is possible to other teachers and students. In providing materials for other staff to use, both the big objective and the stages of development should be clear.

Getting the focus right

Students need help to concentrate on the significant features of an investigation rather than surface features. A debate can easily rage between students on different views of, say, good leisure facilities when the objective is to learn about rights and access to leisure for different groups in the community. It is less to do with what people say than why they say it.

The task is to focus the students on the right kind of thinking by questions, by using appropriate stimulus materials and by a focused conclusion to the activity. Providing a non-expert teacher with a list of prompt questions, which push the students in the right direction, will assist in achieving the planned objectives. They will also need carefully selected materials that give students the opportunity to investigate without finding too many dead ends. Guidance to students should clearly identify the outcomes required in order to keep their agenda clear. This should include reference to both content and skills.

Getting the tasks right

Very open-ended tasks will often lead to little learning if guidance is inadequate in the early stages. Asking KS3 students to investigate the role of the European Union, for example, will probably lead to a pile of printouts from the EU website and little learning.

Investigation should therefore be broken down into bite size sections with clear targets. The work needs to be focused and contextual, with guidance on the most appropriate sources. As skills develop and students become increasingly independent, the targets can become larger and more sophisticated. Members of the Citizenship team will need to be provided with clear guidance on these bite-sized sections if students' investigations are to be successful. To make the most of the time available, groups of students can investigate different sections of a topic and then share their findings.

Differentiating

If all students are to achieve their potential, teaching strategies must be differentiated to meet a variety of needs.

Different information with appropriate prompts should be given to different students. The use of ICT can make this process much easier as it allows materials to be adapted very quickly. This can be done by the Citizenship co-ordinator or allocated to other members of the team. When group tasks are being allocated, students can be given activities which reflect their aptitudes although it is important to help students work on their areas of weakness as well. This can mean pairing students with dissimilar aptitudes so they can learn from each other.

Gathering the evidence

Investigations lead to a great variety of evidence for a student's Citizenship portfolio, all of which contributes to the evidence required for assessment. *The Campaign* led to PowerPoint presentations, reports, displays and witness statements from teachers relating to the contributions of their students.

Students who have taken part in an investigation will have: 'negotiated, decided and taken part in a school or community based activity' as required by the Programme of Study. They will also need to: 'reflect on the process of participating'.

They should therefore be adding a commentary to their work which encourages them to evaluate the activity. For schools using a short course in Citizenship Studies, the record-keeping documents that accompany course work provide a structure for analysis and evaluation. The formula used is helpful for other schools as well.

Helping students to develop skills

Learning to investigate

It is unrealistic to expect students to be adept investigators from the beginning of their school careers. Students' skills need nurturing and will develop with practice.

In the early stages, the Citizenship team can find out about their students' skills by setting tasks which put them into practice at an early stage. Observations on how groups tackle a task, the quality of their reports and their response to key questions will provide insights into students' investigative skills. By building these stages into schemes of work, student profiles can start to develop. As skills are such a critical part of the Citizenship Programme of Study, it is important to establish good practice from an early stage.

Students who are new to the strategy or have had little practice will need the help of clear and frequent guidance. This may also be the case for students who are working in new environments and new contexts.

Coming to their own conclusions

A Citizenship course should allow students to explore their own ideas. In many subject areas, teachers tend to guide students to preconceived answers. In some contexts in which there is a 'right' answer this is entirely appropriate, although it may result in guesswork as students may be more interested in working out the thoughts in the teacher's head than working out the right answer. In Citizenship, however, developing the ability to come to a conclusion based on evidence is an important skill. If members of the Citizenship team are accustomed to working towards the 'right' answer they may need support in helping students to carry out investigative work.

When questioning, it can be difficult to wait while students work out their ideas, so there is a tendency to jump in with the 'right' answer. Planning for students to work together for a few minutes with, perhaps, a series of questions, can help to overcome this problem. Writing this into a scheme of work, provided by the co-ordinator, will help other members of the team to achieve the required outcomes.

Making democratic decisions

What if the students don't like the plans? It is very brave to introduce an activity to the class and go with the flow on finding that students want to do something different. In Citizenship the medium is often the message so helping students to question the questions can play a constructive role in their learning.

As Citizenship is all about learning the skills to manage their own lives, students should be encouraged to discuss objectives and how they will be achieved. An initial discussion with the class about an activity might result in a democratic decision to change the plans. Jettisoning all the plans might be a challenge but discussing adaptations can be built into a scheme of work. This would contribute to students' learning about skills of negotiation as they may not all agree and have to learn to compromise or accept the majority decision.

Developing independent learning

Taking responsibility

It can be difficult to hand over responsibility for organising an investigation. If work is to be genuinely investigative, it must be in the hands of the students, but if they feel it is merely a token gesture, the motivational effects will be dissipated.

Although a structure and framework are essential, by allowing students to organise themselves and plan their work within appropriate parameters, they will start to develop the skills needed for taking responsibility. First efforts may be modest; a group can be given responsibility for choosing how they work with a particular selection of materials, or for choosing some of the criteria by which their results will be judged. Over time, the structure, framework and parameters will become more open as skills develop and responsibility for learning becomes more deeply rooted. This needs to be built into the schemes of work throughout the course.

It is important that regular time is given to students to think about their approach. In any hour's activity, this might be modelled as: 10 minutes of thinking and planning where students contextualise their tasks; 35 minutes of investigation and data-handling; 15 minutes of reflection, of comparing approach and of transferring to new contexts.

In an investigative environment it is important to encourage students without taking away the independence that has been created. Developing the Citizenship team's questioning skills is therefore important. The following framework can be used to underpin such questioning.

The planning stage:

- What are you planning to do and why?
- What will be relevant?
- How will you do it?

Carrying out the investigation:

- Questions or statements to encourage and keep students on task.

Drawing conclusions:

- What did you do and why?
- What would you do differently?
- Was another group's approach more effective?

Keeping students motivated

Motivation can be greatly increased by the use of real investigations as opposed to simulations. As participation plays a significant role in the National Curriculum Programme of Study for Citizenship, students are expected to make a real contribution. There is a variety of strategies for stimulating motivation and therefore engagement.

Using your local area

Is there something that students want to change in the locality? Can they have an influence on decision-making in school or beyond? By rooting investigation in such work, the Citizenship team is not only developing the skills, knowledge and understanding which are required but also creating an environment in which students are likely to be motivated and therefore be more fully engaged.

Setting a realistic challenge

Students are dispirited by failure. In open-ended investigations, they often set themselves objectives that are beyond their reach. It is therefore important to guide the Citizenship team to help students to be realistic in their targets. They are, for example, more likely to persuade the local council to put floodlights on the football pitch than build a whole new sports centre. By providing students with a range of appropriate examples, they are more likely to come up with an achievable challenge.

Success and failure

It is also important for everyone to realise that not all activities will be successful. Community participation of this sort often raises issues which may be rejected initially but sow the seeds of an idea. A student who was involved in setting up a pressure group for a cinema in his town was delighted when, two years later, plans were under discussion. Giving students an example of this sort helps them to realise that while success cannot be guaranteed, they may be influencing the future. In a political context, the suffragettes' story demonstrates the value of a campaign. Many students are unaware that women didn't have the vote.

Resourcing investigation

What resources?

In a perfect world, students would all have access to an Internet-linked computer, a telephone and fax machine in the classroom and a wealth of resources. As the world is never perfect, the use of resources needs to be carefully planned.

- Choose web-based materials that can be downloaded and copied.
- Gather a range of materials as students who are investigating may need a range of information in order to select the most relevant. Some resource centres will collect material related to a topic if given plenty of warning.
- Arrange for groups to be able to use a telephone at specific times. Ensure that they plan their conversation carefully so they don't waste time.
- Collect copies of Yellow Pages. Even old ones are useful.

When Citizenship lessons are in tutor time, pressure can be great as whole year groups or even the whole school can be timetabled at the same time. Ensuring that classes are organised so that they do not bombard individuals or organisations with the same question at the same time will reduce pressure both internally and externally.

Preparing people

Investigations can involve people both in school and beyond. Members of the Citizenship team obviously need to be prepared and well briefed so that they feel secure in helping students to carry out the investigation.

- Detailed lesson plans with guidance about questioning and reminders to let the students answer the questions, for example.
- Adequate resources for their group to meet different needs.
- Involvement in Citizenship planning so they can see the objectives clearly.
- If team members have different areas of expertise a carousel, which allows students to move from teacher to teacher, might enhance the experience for all as students will benefit and teachers will not have to deal with material with which they are not comfortable or interested.

Many schools have resource centres where material can be collected to support topics. Help staff to help support investigation by:

- drawing on their expertise because they will know their existing resources well
- briefing them early so they have time to gather useful material
- giving them clear schedules of when students will be dealing with the topics.

If adults other than teachers are to be involved, they and the students will need guidance. Young people value being listened to, particularly by outsiders. It changes their perspective on the value of the work that has been carried out and gives them confidence in dealing with issues both in and out of school.

The reverse of the coin is that outsiders can get very upset if they are not warned and student motivation can be badly damaged by unfortunate responses. The school where two hundred students decided to phone the council help-line caused distress for all concerned!

- Make sure the objectives of their involvement are clear.
- Check time schedules carefully.
- Ensure that students' phone calls to outside organisations are planned so one individual is not bombarded.

Allocating time

If students are carrying out genuine investigation, they will need time to gather information and work on the responses. The frustration factor can be great for students who are highly motivated by carrying out a 'real' investigation when they find they cannot complete their work effectively because the time has run out. It may be necessary to take a flexible approach to deal with such circumstances.

- Save time by giving groups different areas to investigate. It can also be a good learning experience because students become dependent on each other. A group that has not performed can be under heavy peer group pressure to complete their work when others are depending upon it.

Citizenship activities can put pressure on limited resources so planning the timing of work can be critical.

- A carousel of activities helps people and resources to be used more flexibly. Knowing the pressure points will help to avoid a crisis and assist students to investigate more effectively.

Students sometimes get very involved in a project and want to devote more time to it. The ability of a school to meet this need will depend on the structures that have been set up for Citizenship.

- The 'light touch' of the Citizenship orders means that schools can adapt schedules to meet enthusiasms. This reflects the objectives of the subject and helps students to develop a sense that they can have an effect.

Good investigations

Good investigations should involve the following:

- a topic of interest to the students
- realism
- structure that gives confidence without constraining initiative
- focus on the process of investigation as well as the product
- differentiation to meet the needs of students' skills and abilities
- involvement of people with expertise from outside school
- opportunity to present and discuss outcomes
- debrief to consolidate learning and transferability of knowledge and skills.

Investigation across the curriculum

Business Studies

Investigate a change in the economy and its impact on people and business.

English

Carry out an investigation to support speaking. A wide range of topics can be drawn from the knowledge and understanding section of the Citizenship Programme of Study.

Geography

Group exploration of the local area in Year 7 develops an understanding of the local community. Groups can select different aspects to explore and then share findings.

History

In their study of European or World history, students can investigate an issue or topic from a variety of perspectives.

ICT

Find out about the ethnic diversity in Britain and how migration over the years has happened. Ask questions about why people have migrated into Britain, find a bit about their country of origin, where communities live in Britain, and so on.

Mathematics

An investigation of levels of taxation, national insurance and/or interest rates to develop understanding of percentages.

MFL

Use authentic materials to investigate an aspect of the culture of the country where the target language is spoken.

Music

Investigate the musical culture of another country.

RE

Investigate different aspects of a particular religion or the same aspect of different religions.

Science

Which makes radishes grow better – organic or non-organic fertilisers? http://www.sycd.co.uk/can_we_should_we/pdf/organic_farming/organic_fertiliser.pdf. Related teaching notes can be found at http://www.sycd.co.uk/can_we_should_we/pdf/organic_farming/organic_teach.pdf.

Questions for reflection

- Choose a topic for investigation that combines your own subject knowledge and skills with Citizenship.
- Consider any issues related to the process of investigation including practical matters like the time taken to gather information, access to ICT, pressure on individuals who might be sources of information.
- How will you ensure that the students are aware of the contribution their investigation makes to Citizenship?
- When the investigation is complete, discuss the process with the students. What impact has it had on their learning and skills development?

Chapter 6

Role play

Using perspectives

Why use role play?

Role play asks students to step into someone else's shoes and argue an issue from their point of view. It immerses them in the issue and helps them to develop their cognitive understanding as well as their feelings and values. As a teaching strategy, it fits directly into the Citizenship Programme of Study that expects students at Key Stage 3 to 'use their imagination to consider other people's experiences and be able to think about, express and explain views that are not their own'.

At Key Stage 4, they are also expected to evaluate those views critically.

The context of a role-play activity also encourages students to analyse their own perspectives and values. This combines effectively with the Citizenship Programme of Study as many issues are sensitive and ask students to address their own values. Role play helps them to develop a personal meaning and to work out dilemmas with the help of others in the group. A problem is defined, acted out, discussed and conclusions reached in the light of other people's points of view. Even if there is no final agreement, students are learning that a rationale is needed to justify any point of view.

The emotional element in role play contributes to later analysis. The student, who becomes completely wrapped up in a role, learns to appreciate that people's actions have an emotional as well as a rational content. It is important to realise that in issues that are influenced by attitudes, values and perceptions, the emotional and rational content are often closely intertwined and have to be untangled if students are to evaluate effectively. In Science, for example, the question of animal testing is an issue that is close to the heart of many teenagers. They find it hard to untangle the emotional and rational arguments so role play can assist them in working out both sides of the story.

Through role play students can . . .

- explore their feelings
- gain insights into their attitudes, values and perceptions
- explore subject matter in varied ways.

(Joyce *et al.* 1997)

Being able to move into a different persona can make it easier for students to consider their own and other people's views on an issue. The 'third-party' experience of taking on and discussing issues within a role provides a safer setting than having to talk directly about a personal experience. When students are provided with cards or other guidance on a role, it helps them take this third-party position.

Being asked to take on a role that contradicts their own point of view means that students have to work out the rationale from another perspective. This is a powerful strategy because they are often willing to discount other people's perspectives as irrational.

Playing a role involves the whole person. When body, mind and voice are all committed to the activity, students become immersed in a way that most activities do not allow. As a result, their thought processes can become more sensitive to the attitudes of the person whose role they are playing.

The objective of a role-play activity is often to solve a problem that involves both personal and interpersonal issues. Students are therefore being asked to put a rational construct on personal perspectives. Having to think through arguments from different perspectives prepares students to 'negotiate, decide and take part responsibly in both school and community based activities' as the Citizenship Programme of Study requires. All these ways in which role play can be used help to develop a sense of empathy so students do not just discount other people's views, issues and values as invalid.

Published role-play activities are available for many subjects and, because they inevitably include a variety of perspectives, they frequently provide an excellent way of incorporating Citizenship into the curriculum.

Running role play

Scale

Role play can be used for quick activities with a short preparation period to start a train of thought. Students think about introductory ideas and raise questions but go on to consider the issues in more depth in other ways. It can also be used on a larger scale as the core of the lesson with more preparation time and more sophisticated debriefing.

Stages of a role play

- Warm up the group
- Select participants
- Set the scene
- Prepare observers
- Enact
- Discuss and evaluate
- Re-enact
- Discuss and evaluate
- Share experiences and generalise

(Shaftel and Shaftel 1967)

The stages described by Shaftel and Shaftel (1967) show the process for a larger-scale activity. The idea of re-enacting is a useful strategy because it gives students an opportunity to respond to the debriefing and evaluation. A quick role play which asks students to think about introductory ideas in order to raise some questions will run through the same pattern but may not go through the stage of re-enacting because students go on to consider the issues in different ways.

A larger-scale activity may need two lessons to give time for planning and preparation. In the initial lesson, the first four stages can take place with groups of students developing the ideas for each role. If observers are being used, they need guidance to help them develop the questions that they want answered.

In the second lesson, the role play takes place along with any subsequent discussion. Participants must understand both the objectives of the role play and the ground rules so that the outcomes of the activity are clear. The discussion and evaluation at the end allow students to step back out of role. Questions from teachers and peers can help to debrief students and allow for a cooling-off period if emotions are running high.

The move to generalisation is important because this is where students learn to transfer ideas from the personal and familiar to new contexts. In Citizenship this is extremely important because students are learning to deal with values in the context of knowledge and understanding. A role play in Science or Geography which does not take this step often will not be recognised by students as applicable to life in general.

Techniques

Role-play activities can use either a fishbowl technique in which one group performs for the rest or a multiple approach in which several are run in parallel. If several groups are being run at the same time, they might all be working on the same story, related ones or completely different ones. Whichever approach is chosen, the feedback and discussion afterwards is where much of the learning takes place so needs to be carefully planned.

Some activities, such as Designing a New Yoghurt (Wellington 1994), combine both strategies. Students first work in pairs in the role of corporate scientists and then as members of the board of the company to make a decision about which yoghurt to produce. The first part operates as a 'multiple approach', the latter is convened as a fishbowl activity.

The audience participation format, in which a presenter raises an issue and then has conversations with individuals who hold different points of view in order to generate discussion, is a useful activity for role play. It is familiar to students as it is used in many television programmes and is therefore a context where students have seen a range of perspectives offered and discussed. The format also allows the teacher in the role of the presenter to control the pace and direction of the activity if this is seen as desirable.

Themes and rules

It is tempting to devise role-play activities which transport students into realms which are unfamiliar. This needs to be done with caution because, without enough background experience, students' contributions may be of little value. Role play is more worthwhile when information is provided and students are then able to deal with the situation with some personal insight. The Science role play on the design of a new yoghurt, for example, deals with a product students know well, the concept of what customers might want and Science they have worked on. From this combination of understanding and experience, they can move to the less familiar decision-making role as a board of directors.

Whatever the theme, one rule that is helpful is to work strictly with the information provided. Role cards and information sheets need to contain any information that will be required. Problems are easy to solve and arguments easy to win when participants are allowed to invent their own information so 'magical' solutions become possible. Keeping students' feet on the ground is therefore important if the role play is to work and students can face up to real-life constraints.

Taking on a role

All students at Key Stage 3 should be able to 'justify orally and in writing a personal opinion about such issues, problems or events' and 'contribute to group and exploratory class discussions, and take part in debates'.

When setting up role play, all students need to be encouraged to take a range of roles over a period of time. A class can get tired of hearing the voice of students who always want to be in the limelight. More diffident students may take less prominent roles initially but should be coaxed into leading groups and reporting as time passes. The role of observer who feeds back outcomes to the whole group is often a useful development role for less confident students. In general, students take a responsible attitude to other's learning experiences.

Some roles are less familiar to students than others and so provide a more challenging proposition to take on. Through a scheme of work, a student may be asked to play, for example, the roles of a fellow teenager, a parent, an environmentalist and a politician.

In order to develop the sensitivity to other people's views that Citizenship tries to develop, students should be encouraged to try out roles, including those which contradict their own perspectives. Learning to develop empathy is the result.

Learning with role play

What is a role?

In everyday life each individual has a set of characteristics which underpins the roles that they take. Even if they play different roles in different situations, which many of us do, these characteristics give each role common features.

People also interpret the roles that others play in everyday life from their own perspective so any human interaction is going to be influenced by these characteristics.

This complexity means that, in order to build the sensitivity to other people's views that Citizenship tries to develop, students should be encouraged to try out roles in safe situations, including those that contradict their own perspectives. Learning to develop empathy is the result.

A role-play activity contains a range of aspects, all of which need careful thought if students are to derive real benefit. The ingredients of a good role play include:

- the problem
- the contribution of different characters and their motives
- the analysis
- the solution
- the evaluation of the solution from the perspectives of the different characters.

Students have to be fully aware of the objectives of the activity and the various influences at work within it. If they can explain how and why the solution to a problem affects individuals and explain the balance of the trade-offs between people, the activity will have contributed considerably to their knowledge, skills and understanding.

Cross-curricular learning

In many schools Citizenship is taught in a cross-curricular context. Lessons often combine the development of subject knowledge with activities that help to develop Citizenship skills. There is an added advantage when an activity encourages both subject and Citizenship knowledge and understanding.

In Science, a long-established role-play activity involves the design, marketing and selling of a new yoghurt. Students learn about the science involved in making and eating yoghurt at Key Stage 4. This activity also engages with the Citizenship Programme of Study's requirement for students to understand 'how the economy functions, including the role of business'.

Students take different roles including market researchers, yoghurt scientist and marketing advisers. They act as a board of directors that develops and presents its strategy to the rest of the class. The activity offers students the opportunity to learn their science in a way that engages with the world at large.

As students often feel worried about getting the wrong answer, this activity provides a context in which science understanding is developed, students are asked to produce their own ideas and there is no wrong or right answer.

Science and Citizenship

> The life skills aspect of scientific and technological problem solving is also important. Not only do we live in a culture dominated by science and technology, but the information and knowledge it generates are too vast to be assimilated by students. Furthermore they are increasing at an astonishing rate. Students will therefore need a wide range of learning skills to cope with this increase. The ability to recognise problems in a broad range of contexts, understand their nature and plan, execute and evaluate solutions will be central to these skills and of vital importance to citizens of the twenty-first century.
>
> (Wellington 1994)

Many cross-curricular role-play activities help students to develop empathy. *President for a Day* (see Chapter 9) asks students to put themselves into the shoes of the president of a less economically developed country. In Chapter 4, students are asked to consider the role of people during the Industrial Revolution. These activities engage the students in interesting contexts, but they often need help to transfer their understanding from the subject-based focus to their own present-day environment and genuine Citizenship.

Active learning

Role play is a kinaesthetic activity and facilitates learning for students in a particular way. Using it as a strategy in a scheme of work therefore helps to meet the needs of all students. It provides a manageable context where body language, movement around the classroom and mixing in different groups are all a legitimate part of classroom learning. In preparation for their presentations (Chapter 8), students in various roles had the option to meet other groups to form pressure groups. The movement and mix of students generated an exciting groundswell of ideas enjoyed by all.

Although it is important to give students opportunities to take all sorts of parts in role play if they are to develop the skills required in Citizenship, the mix of audience, reporter and contributor provides a range of activities which offer every student a valuable experience.

Many students lack assertiveness whereas others have an excess. By encouraging the less assertive to participate, they can develop confidence in a safe environment. Role play does not always draw the noisy individuals to the forefront because it requires a combination of constructive thought that gives confidence and the willingness to contribute.

Creative role play

Creativity and Citizenship

Citizenship is not only about what is but also about what might be. Can we imagine a better, fairer and more successful society? What would that world be like? How might it be created?

(Fisher 2003)

Citizenship is aiming to create a better future by encouraging young people to participate and take a constructive role in society. Many young people assume that the world they see is a given and expect to have little influence. If students have the opportunity to explore that adult world free of constraints, they may come up with solutions that are outside current experience. This helps them to understand that change is possible, particularly if they are encouraged to participate.

Although role play needs some constraints to avoid ludicrous suggestions for the future, it can take away existing boundaries. Role play allows students to brainstorm solutions to a problem, as they do not have to assume the mental and practical constraints of older people. Local councillors have been surprised when asked into schools to contribute to such activities because of the willingness of students to think 'out of the box'.

The combination of creativity and the enthusiasm of young people to get things done can lead to some exciting outcomes – particularly in the field of active Citizenship.

Motivating role play

Role play is often different and fun. Students have to work together, plan, work out how to be persuasive and present their point of view. All these activities are part of the skills of Citizenship, which, when combined with a fun experience, helps students to remember, not only the context of the activity but also their contributions.

Because individuals take specific roles or represent their group, students are learning autonomy, a crucial skill if they are to become effective citizens. Young people who are prepared to stand up for their beliefs and challenge others have a considerable degree of personal autonomy.

Successful role play

The success of role play depends on the way in which it takes place and the analysis and evaluation of the outcomes. When students make a personal investment in the activity and therefore feel committed to the process, the outcomes are likely to have considerable benefits. This may take some time to perfect as performing a role and taking on another character are not second nature to everyone. It is therefore wise to start with a simple problem and roles that are not too complex and move to more sophisticated models as students become more at ease with the strategy.

The selection of topics and roles needs to be made carefully to ensure that the activity is within the scope of the students involved if learning outcomes are going to be worthwhile. Students could discuss, for example, the view that stealing from a large store is not as bad as stealing from a friend. A short role play between a shopkeeper and a child accused of stealing could be the start of a lesson. A more elaborate role play could explore causes and consequences of stealing from large stores. Roles would include supermarket managers, other shoppers, insurance companies, security staff and perhaps people who own shares in the company that owns the supermarket.

Case study: role play for Citizenship in KS3 English

The school

Christopher Whitehead School is an 11–16 comprehensive in Worcester. Citizenship appears as a discrete subject on the timetable alongside PSHE lessons but other subjects teach Citizenship issues where they match National Curriculum Programmes of Study.

In the English Key Stage 3 programme there are many controversial topics that provide good contexts for speaking, reading and writing. Bullying in school is one such issue; students have many different views about the nature of bullying, the contexts in which it takes place and what should best be done about it by students and by adults.

In this case study, a group of Year 8 students explores the responsibilities of different people involved in a bullying incident. This lesson follows work on empathy where students had been asked to think about a variety of 'problems' in the role of a magazine 'agony aunt'.

The lesson will be followed up by further work on school responses to bullying incidents and the link between 'standing up for what is right' in the community as well as in school.

The lesson

Commentary

Aims

- To empathise with one person's view of a bullying incident.
- To identify similarities and differences in people's views towards bullying.
- To understand the reasons behind individual and school views of bullying.

Students have spent several lessons where they are asked to put themselves in other people's shoes. This lesson draws on their own personal experiences but focuses on a third party through role play. Students will be asked to act out their ideas and to explain their views in role through 'hot seating'. A further whole-class summary of 'the best way of dealing with the incident' is used as a way of 'debriefing' when the role play is completed

Background and content

Role cards provide different background information for up to six key participants. A Year 8 boy has supposedly been the subject of bullying by other students in and out of school. The student playing the form tutor has an important role in initiating discussion. The form tutor has a background information sheet but is asked to try to draw out views from the group.

The class has experienced little role play together in English at this point so they will need to be helped into the process. The teacher has identified five strong individuals to take the part of the form tutor, in each group.

The role cards have been prepared with just sufficient information to help students but without the need for time to be spent on comprehension tasks.

The starter

Students sit in a large circle and take turns to ask each other questions across the circle about the last lesson. The emphasis is on quick questions and answers with lots of praise from the teacher, particularly for anyone who showed empathy towards other people's views.

The emphasis here is on taking part and praise is given for 'having a go' rather than for any particular content.

The circle of chairs is made as small as possible to help students feel they are part of a tight-knit group with a shared purpose.

The idea of empathy is important for today's lesson.

Students are then asked to form five groups around named individuals. The ground rules for the discussion groups include

- follow instructions on the briefing card
- be sympathetic towards anyone who is upset. (10 minutes)

A very limited class briefing is given about the actual bullying incident because students have to find out from each other what has happened. Partial information is often the reality in school.

The core: role play in groups

The student role-playing the form tutor asks others in their group what they know about a story that John has been bullied. The details of the bullying episodes build as different students add their explanations drawn from their briefing cards and from their own experiences.

The teacher checks that each group is on task and occasionally asks a direct question of the participants. (20 minutes)

The role cards give some reluctant students a cue.

Matching appropriate cards to certain students can be important. Some cards have a specific gender role; others are open to interpretation.

Confident 'form tutors' ask questions and quickly spot some contradictions between accounts.

Some groups act more spontaneously and it can become a free-for-all.

Some students find they have little idea and swap role cards. Some students prefer to work as a pair.

The teacher intervenes where the rules are broken (one student becoming intolerant with another) and in one case, asks questions of different participants to encourage more talk.

Hot seating

After a short moment of quiet when students are asked to think about what has been said and how they have carried out their roles, the class is reorganised to face six chairs at the front.

Students from each group who have played a particular role are called out in

This process helps students to think about both the outcomes of their role play and the ways in which they have interpreted the roles.

Those in the 'hot seat' are answering questions in role; the remainder of the class can ask questions out of role and turn to sit in a set of 'hot seats' where they can make a brief statement about their experience and be asked questions 'in role'.

Different views of the nature and cause of the bullying emerge from some of the groups. (15 minutes)

can begin to see similarities and differences in the way roles have been played. The teacher is in a position to ask questions which may deepen understanding or pick up on additional issues.

The order in which the different 'roles' are explored can be important. The form tutors have had more information than others and a more active role initially. It may be wise to leave them to last in this stage.

The 'cooling down' time that this stage offers is important if students have empathised strongly with particular roles.

Plenary

The teacher asks the whole class to think about the bullying episode out of role. Key questions are used to serve as a bridge between the role play and events which may occur for real in school.

What do you think should now happen?

Who, if anyone, is to blame?

What is your responsibility in such episodes?

What should the school do about the situation?

The teacher finishes by underlining two points: the importance of understanding other people's viewpoints through role play and the link between responsible behaviour as a student in school and behaviour as a member of the community out of school. (15 minutes)

This stage offers the opportunity to link the students' experience in the lesson to the school's policy towards bullying and to similar episodes experienced perhaps by students and adults in families, at work and in the community at large.

Students often have a strong sense of 'justice needs to be done' and find a school policy hard to understand if it pursues a 'no blame' approach to bullying. This can be a good way of thinking about why a school reaction differs to that of an individual.

The time for plenaries can easily be squeezed. In this case, it is important that students have the time, either in class or as an individual study task, to think about the incident from a different perspective.

Resources

John's story provides the background to the bullying incident but isn't made available to the group until later on in the activity. Each student is given a role card telling them about the part they will play.

John's story

JOHN has transferred from another school into Year 8 and he does not know anyone at his new school. He has moved because his younger brother has kidney problems and the family needs to be nearer to the hospital where his brother is treated. John is really worried about his brother but doesn't want to talk about it. He is good at football and used to play for a team. He doesn't feel like joining in the lunchtime football games or sharing the jokes of other students.

Some of the tutor group have made fun of John for not joining in and they often call him names. John thinks two of them have been following him home and one of them, SAM, threw John's bag at him after PE, hitting him in the face and scraping his cheek badly.

John now really worries about going to school and wishes he had not left his old friends.

Role card: John's form tutor

You are John's Year 8 FORM TUTOR. You are worried about John because he seems to be getting more and more quiet and withdrawn.

You sit him next to ROB who is very good at football because John's last school report said that he played for a local team. The two boys seem to ignore each other and Rob has asked to move several times.

You are waiting to meet John's parents at the open evening next week.

You have just been told by a girl in the tutor group that Sam threw a bag at John and that 'everyone has been bullying him'. John has a large scrape down his face.

Role card: Rob – a boy in John's class

You are in Year 8. You think that the new boy, JOHN, is very strange. He has not made friends and never seems to talk to anyone about himself or his family.

You live in the next road to him and often walk home the same way. He always stays ahead of you and never says hello, so now you avoid talking to him.

You have noticed that some others in the class have been picking on him and calling him names but you have not said anything.

A group at work

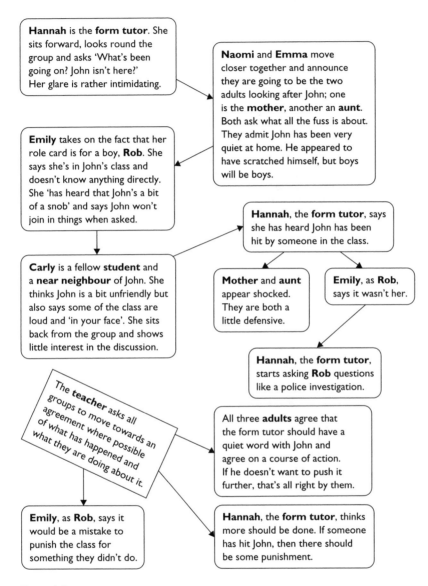

Figure 6.1

Hot seating

The students who played the same role in each group were brought together to share their responses in front of the class. See Figures 6.2 and 6.3.

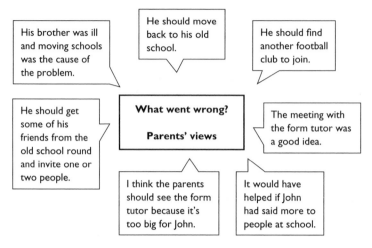

Figure 6.2

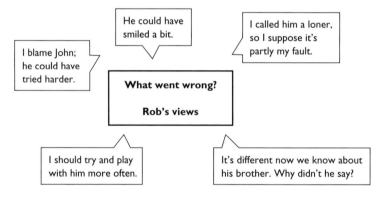

Figure 6.3

The plenary

See Figure 6.4.

Reflection

The class involved in this activity had not been involved in role play before so it took a while to become accustomed to the approach. Inevitably some groups needed more support than others. The role of form tutor had been carefully allocated to students who were more confident because they had to look at the issue from all perspectives. The teacher felt that they would have benefited from a group discussion of the role so that everyone could see the issues involved.

Figure 6.4 The Plenary

I blame John; he could have tried harder.

Hot seating drew together the ideas of people who were looking at the problem from the same perspective. It proved particularly useful because the class could see how even people looking at the problem from the same perspective might have different views.

It's different now we know about his brother. Why didn't he say?

The art of Citizenship teaching is to draw students' personal experiences and their classroom experience into an appreciation of the realities of the world. Allowing more time for this and considering carefully how it might occur provides the

I need more time to make the links to the outside world. There were a few, more mature students who had a ready understanding; the others probably need a specific case study, say of bullying at work, to make the links.

It was fun and some students really came to the fore. We will do this again and I think other departments could readily use roles to explore issues.

link. The teacher recognised that on a future occasion, this aspect of the lesson would benefit from more attention. A further lesson would give these opportunities.

Developing Citizenship understanding

Role play is often used to deal with conflict situations. It helps students to see a problem from several perspectives, while distancing them from the personal aspects.

The main contribution this activity makes to the knowledge aspect of citizenship is therefore the development of understanding of 'the importance of resolving conflict fairly.' It also starts to introduce the idea of 'the need for mutual respect and understanding'.

Students are, in this activity, working in a familiar context that can later be transferred to the wider issues of 'the diversity of national, regional, religious and ethnic identities in the United Kingdom'.

The teacher identified the need to help students make the link from the activity and their own experience to how schools deal with bullying and the contribution that students can make to improve their community. Once these ideas of conflict resolution have been discussed the ideas can be revisited in broader contexts.

Developing Citizenship skills

Role play helps students develop a range of Citizenship skills because it asks them to look at problems from different perspectives by standing in other people's shoes so they must 'use their imagination to consider other people's experiences and be able to think about, express and explain views that are not their own'.

This activity asks them to see the world from perspectives that are familiar and therefore makes a good introduction to role play. Some students find it difficult to start participating in role play so they are likely to find it difficult to work in this way in real situations. The activity provides the opportunity to practice the skills in a non-threatening environment.

In order to develop the role play, students are asked to 'contribute to group and exploratory class discussions' and then 'justify orally and in writing a personal opinion about such issues, problems or events'.

Once the activity has moved beyond the actual role play to discuss how a school might deal with bullying, students are being asked to consider how to 'negotiate, decide and take part responsibly in both school and community based activities' and 'reflect on the process of participating'.

Bullying makes a good starting point for discussions of 'topical political, spiritual, moral, social and cultural issues, problems and events' because many such problems, when explored at a personal level, involve one group of individuals bullying another.

Role play across the curriculum

Business Studies

A public inquiry provides a good vehicle for role play in Business Studies. The topic can be related to the local community or a bigger national or international issue. The role of stakeholders combined with ethical issues make the links with Citizenship explicit.

Design and Technology

Students have to evaluate their products in terms of the needs of the customer, fitness for purpose, global and environmental impact and how it compares with other people's products. Using role play will help them to see these perspectives in a practical way and apply the skills to their own projects.

Geography

A role play that explored different perspectives on the location of a wind farm or other environmental issue will help students to develop an understanding of how such developments can affect different people in different ways and how individuals may have conflicting interests.

History

A role-play activity that explored soldiers signing on and leaving from the Second World War gives students the opportunity to explore a range of perspectives on conflict.

MFL

Role play in MFL can help students to develop the ability to express themselves in the target language. The topic of the role play can be related to culture or a current event. The school community can also be the basis for role play. Bullying has been discussed in the context of English but could equally well be used in MFL.

RE

A role play could investigate how an individual whose life was centred around a religious vocation affected other people and the community.

Science

Global warming – time for action? The class is arranged into small groups of three or four students. Each group is given a role card with information about one person's view, with room for specific details to be added by the group: English farmer, Manchester tourist board official, a keen amateur sportsperson from Boulder, Colorado, Bangladeshi government official, West African novelist, UK electricity company salesperson, international oil company representative and UN official. Groups get into role, then one person from each group plays out his or her character's perceptions and ideas, aiming for authentic and dramatic presentations. One student chairs the proceedings. Remaining students play a TV studio audience. Time is allowed for a class discussion after everyone has stepped out of role, to review what happened and why.

Questions for reflection

Think of a topic you teach where different perspectives play an important part.

- How could a role-play activity be used to help students understand different viewpoints?
- How could you use role play to promote enjoyable learning and Citizenship in your subject?
- How do your teaching colleagues use role-play activities? Are there opportunities to work together using role play to promote Citizenship skills and understanding?
- Discuss with colleagues who have experience of role play how best to assess students' contributions. How might students' work appear in Citizenship profiles?

Chapter 7

Group work
Strategies and outcomes

Why work in groups?

Collaborative learning means working together, respecting other people's points of view and coming to a democratic conclusion. These are all skills that Citizenship aims to develop. As evidence shows that group work enhances learning, there are powerful reasons to use it in the classroom.

Learning democratically

Working in groups helps students to develop a democratic context for learning. By practising making collaborative decisions, students are developing habits that should make the transition to larger scale democratic processes more straightforward.

In Citizenship this might involve coming to a joint conclusion when selecting an activity to undertake and then deciding who will take each role. Establishing rules for group work provides a framework for such discussion and decision-making.

Developing social skills

Group work facilitates the development of interpersonal intelligence (Gardner 1985) because students have to learn together. This involves negotiating with others who may have a different point of view and coming to conclusions as a group. A group is a small, safe, unit to practise in both for the confident student and others who are less willing to participate. Having watched others contribute to discussion, a less confident student may become more willing to have a go. Peer group pressure also means that individual students take their contribution seriously because they will be letting the group down if they don't.

Developing cognitive skills

Solving problems is often the objective of group work. To achieve results, students have to work out exactly what they mean and explain concepts and ideas to others.

In Citizenship, arriving at a shared meaning of terms such as rights, responsibilities and fairness, is important if further discussion is to be meaningful.

Providing emotional support

Group work has a motivational effect because students are working together on a common problem. This often creates an environment in which people are prepared to play their part and try out ideas because they feel secure in a smaller community. Where groups are competing with each other or contributing to a whole class activity, the same applies.

In Citizenship a student might be happy to discuss the different identities that make them an individual in the context of a small group but not in a whole class. These identities might include ethnic background, religion, club membership or how they spent their leisure time.

Learning efficiently

More can be achieved if tasks are shared. If the class as a whole is working on a big problem, groups can take responsibility for different parts of the activity, as in *The Campaign* (see Chapter 5). This allows a class to take on a bigger challenge. Alternatively, groups can work on similar tasks in order to generate discussion about different approaches or provide a competitive edge.

There is a danger that students may, within a group, select activities that they know they can do. The jigsaw (Slavin 1983) is a well-established strategy for group work. It helps to structure group work so students practise all the skills, not just those in which they already have expertise.

In Citizenship students might work on different information about asylum seekers in order to create a resource for the whole class.

The objectives of Citizenship teaching and the objectives of using group work have much in common as the quote from Whitaker (1995) suggests.

Small group work:

- creates a climate in which students can work with a sense of security and self-confidence
- facilitates the growth of understanding by offering the optimum opportunity for students to talk reflectively with each other
- promotes a spirit of co-operation and mutual respect.

(Whitaker 1995)

The development of young people who can, and want to participate as citizens has roots in the confidence that grows through group work. The willingness to listen to other people's point of view is an integral part of developing the skills required for group work. These skills together build the foundations for working within a democratic process.

Working in groups

Group work provides interaction between teachers and students in a variety of ways. Students talk with each other while focusing on the task. The teacher can communicate with the whole class, a group as a whole or with individual group members according to planning or the development of the lesson.

Group structure and organisation will affect the quality of this interaction and the likely learning outcomes so it is important to establish the objectives clearly.

Teacher and group interaction

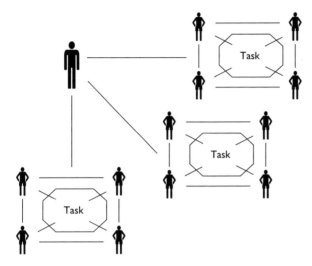

Figure 7.1

Group size

The size of groups will obviously depend on the nature of the task. For a general discussion or brainstorm, four seems to be the most effective number. It also allows for pairs within groups. Three or five or more often means that someone gets left out but can be helpful if a clear decision is required. Some activities have been devised to suit groups of specific sizes. These include negotiation exercises in which students work in pairs or a public inquiry where a number of different points of view are required. Classes don't often turn up with the exact number of students to fit the groups, so a flexible approach is essential. Using an observer who records discussion and summarises the views of the group often helps to overcome the numbers problem. It may also be useful to pair students to support a weak group member.

Group composition

Groups can be put together in different ways. The simplest is to allow friendship groups to work together. This is particularly helpful when students need trust and confidence in each other to discuss sensitive issues like identity. The drawback to this is that students do not learn to work with people from different groupings. The students working on *President for a Day* (see Chapter 9) observed that their friends often held the same point of view on issues. It is therefore worth establishing the practice of mixing student groups on a regular basis.

Research (Bennett 1991) suggests that mixed ability groups lead to highest achievement all round, provided that high attaining students are also given opportunities to work together. This reinforces the argument for changing groups for different activities.

The mix of boys and girls can affect the dynamics of a group because boys tend to be more willing to contribute but girls generally make more thoughtful contributions.

Students with prior experience of a subject can make a valuable contribution to group work. It is therefore worth considering building groups around them to add value to discussions.

Working in groups provides benefits for the development of Citizenship skills as well as subject learning. Students who learn to work effectively with everyone in the class will have gained the ability to listen to and evaluate different points of view as well as expressing their own.

Group rules

In a Citizenship class, learning to establish a framework of rules to organise the way a group will work provides an understanding of how and why society needs rules. The establishment of the rules makes an effective introduction to group work. Each group can draw up a list and agree it. Each list is shared with the class and students are asked to justify their selection. A definitive list is then drawn up democratically and the list is then displayed for future use.

Group tasks

Groups lend themselves to a variety of different sorts of tasks.

Brainstorming and discussion

Brainstorming and discussion mean students are asked to investigate or discuss an issue. This can be used at various points in a lesson. A snappy starter can get a class to pull out the main ideas for development in the rest of the lesson. In a longer time period students might be asked to put together an argument for or against an issue. A lesson might finish with groups rounding up the ideas that have been developed.

Solving problems

Solving problems is a key activity in Citizenship because the subject is full of problems that students need to consider in order to draw conclusions. Once they have been provided with plenty of information to draw upon, groups can work out the pros and cons of various solutions. A government has to decide how to spend the revenue from taxes. Students might be asked to prioritise. By doing it in a group, each individual has to appreciate that others have different points of view and to learn to think about the range of perspectives.

On a larger scale, the group might be organising a school event. In these circumstances, students have to plan and decide who does what as well as monitoring the outcomes.

This type of group work can be used to develop understanding of Citizenship content as well as encouraging participation.

Making things

Making things happens most effectively in groups. Understanding what business does or development issues can be effectively carried out by group activities that involve making things – especially if students are asked to work out how the processes should be carried out.

Learning in groups

Classes are often organised into groups but this does not always mean that students are engaging in collaborative learning. If students are closely following instructions and feeding back results, as often happens in a Science practical session, they are not involved in discussion or consideration of why things are happening and the effects of the outcomes. In the context of Citizenship, group work and collaborative learning contribute to the Programme of Study, both as a way of developing an understanding of the content as well as the skills.

In order to achieve effective collaborative learning, it is important to understand the processes involved and how learning is taking place.

A teacher's role is to:

- facilitate progress with the task
- intervene when necessary to direct energies towards the outcomes
- help students develop personal understanding from the activity.

These points may happen before, during and after the group activity has taken place. Intervention should be kept to a minimum and should be sensitive to the way the group is working. It is important to be flexible because groups may not always respond in the expected way. The objectives are to develop the skills identified in the introduction to the chapter.

Developing group work skills

In order to learn in groups, students need to develop a range of skills.

Skills for group work

- the ability to understand the needs of others and take turns
- the ability to articulate a point of view
- the ability to listen to the viewpoint of others
- the ability to respond, question, discuss, argue and reason.

(Fisher 1995)

The development of these skills is not instinctive. Some students want to dominate while others are loath to contribute at all. The natural leaders may tend to do all the work while others sit back. The combination of bite-sized activities for practice, teacher intervention and the rules established by the students themselves can overcome these issues.

The conversation about the way the local council spends its money shows how students can indulge in 'pub talk'. The initial phase involves two students who merely throw their own views at each other. They haven't been listening to each other. When a third member of the group enters the discussion, the direction changes. He has been listening to what the others have had to say, built on their views and proposed an idea that leads to a solution to the dispute.

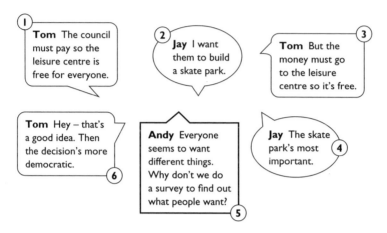

Figure 7.2

Who's listening and thinking?

One strategy that helps students to develop this process of listening and thinking is to ask them to repeat the point of view of the last person before adding their own comment.

If group members take turns to be the observer or reporter they also learn to listen and have the opportunity to take a more reflective view of the discussion.

What are students doing?

When working in groups, students can be doing a variety of things.

- They may each be involved in individual tasks that contribute to a group outcome. The tasks may have been allocated by the teacher or sorted out among the group members. In the early stages, it may be more straightforward to allocate the roles but as students become more skilled, the allocation of activities contributes to Citizenship development.
- They may be working together on an activity with a joint outcome. In this case, the group is focused on one task. There may, however, be tasks to be carried out by individuals within the group. Who is recording the outcomes? Who will present the findings? Is someone creating a presentation?
- They may be working together on a task which contributes to a joint outcome. If the whole class is planning a major activity, like running a disco or planning an outing, groups may have specific areas of responsibility. Peer group pressure can be a source of motivation because the rest of the class will be unhappy if one group hasn't pulled its weight.

When group work is carefully designed to achieve clear outcomes, students can gain a sound understanding of the knowledge, skills and understanding included in the Citizenship Programme of Study. Social and cognitive skills are developed in the context of an emotionally supportive environment.

Learning from evaluation

Evaluation is a critical element of group work whether it has been based within the group or as a contribution to a whole class activity.

Students should have the opportunity to reflect on what they have learnt and how effectively the group has worked. By considering these aspects together, they can draw their own conclusions about the knowledge and skills expected from the activity.

Case study: Citizenship in KS3 Science

The school

Drayton School, Banbury, is an 11–16 mixed comprehensive school where Citizenship is taught in the context of PSHE and across the curriculum.

This Science lesson took place with a mixed ability Year 7 class. The context of the Bottom Paper Tester's Office caused considerable amusement and provided a good background for learning about mass and force as well as developing an understanding of how a business must budget if it is to be successful.

The lesson	Commentary

Aims

- To apply the concept of mass and force.
- To introduce ideas of budgeting.
- To introduce the concept of voting.

Background and content

The classroom became the Office of the Bottom Paper Tester for this lesson. Students were greeted by an official-looking notice on the door regarding its change of status. The Year 7 group had done some preparatory work in mass and force. They were now ready to put the ideas to work. They were to work out how to test the paper themselves.	The class was obviously used to working in a humorous environment and engaged with the context most effectively.

The starter

The teacher set the scene and explained that the task was to test 'bottom paper' to see which would work most effectively.

The class was then quizzed on some of the ideas that were to be used.

The core

Students worked in groups made up of the Boss, who was in charge of the money, the Scientist, who organised the testing, and the Technical Writer, who laid down the rules about how the team worked. Having created some rules, the group voted on the proposals. Each team was given a budget of £5 to spend. Each person cost the group 50p per day, which was collected as a tax, water cost 50p per 100 ml and spare paper was 50p per strip.

The groups were provided with a tray to contain water, some strips of different coloured 'bottom paper' and some weights.

They used these to test each type of paper in order to decide which was most effective.

Once testing was complete, each group had to work out the cost of their activities and discover whether they were within budget.

The teacher moved from group to group giving encouragement and advice where necessary. On the whole, little support was needed as the class was on task and keen to achieve their outcomes at the minimum cost.

The plenary

Each group reported its test outcomes and financial situation. The teacher divulged the makes of the paper so the students could align the outcomes with their memory of the adverts on television. There was then some discussion on the difference between the messages from the adverts and reality.

Review

The class established their groups quickly and sorted out the roles each individual was to take. Under the guidance of the Technical Writer, they came up with plans to carry out the activity. This was concluded by a vote on the potential strategies in order to select the one that each group would run with.

When asked about why they were trying to save money, most of the students had a concept of budgeting that related to their personal finances and hadn't considered the idea in the context of a business or organisation.

> It's Mothers' Day soon.

> Going down town.

Many of them knew about saving and why they did it.

> I don't have enough money so I have to save it for things I want like CDs and games.

Some were starting to see that it was important for the Office of the Bottom Paper Tester not to waste money because there were costs involved in the process.

> Don't use too much water – we've got to pay for other things!

> We mustn't waste money because we have to pay people and buy stuff.

The tax collector went round each group to collect the tax that was to be paid on each member of the group. They all duly paid up but when questioned about taxes in general, members of the class knew very little. They didn't realise that they were taxpayers and had little idea about what taxes were for. Neither VAT nor income tax elicited a response. This reinforces research evidence about young people's lack of knowledge and understanding of the role of taxation in government and the economy (Davies *et al.* 2002).

When questioned about their attitude to working in groups, all students responded very positively. They felt that sharing ideas enhanced the outcomes.

> We all had a go at testing the paper and checked that everyone did it properly.

> We worked out how to test the paper. We all put in our ideas and decided on the best.

They shared ideas, decided on the best way of doing things and acted as quality control on each other.

> I'm sure I'll remember about forces and mass 'cos we all worked together on it.

Students felt that the combination of group work and the context of the activity meant that they would remember what they'd learnt.

> I'm bound to remember about forces and mass because we were in the Office of the Bottom Paper Tester.

Developing Citizenship understanding

The class successfully used a process of voting to decide on their strategy for carrying out the tests. They were, as a result, developing some understanding of the expectation of the Citizenship Programme of Study on 'the importance of voting'.

Students had an initial encounter with ideas of budgeting in a different context from their experience of personal finance. This is really laying the foundations for Citizenship at Key Stage 4 when they are expected to develop an understanding of the way businesses work.

The Programme of Study asks students to develop an understanding of 'central and local government, the public services they offer and how they are financed, and the opportunities to contribute'.

The lesson touched on these ideas but students needed considerable further work to turn the experience into understanding.

Developing Citizenship skills

Every member of the class was 'contributing to group and exploratory class discussions'.

They worked effectively together and no groups appeared to be unable to plan, carry out the activity and come to conclusions.

The activity itself was mainly aimed at developing Science understanding with a Citizenship thread running through it. The students were also developing the skills they need for Citizenship by learning to work together and share ideas.

Reflection

The humour of the activity clearly had a strong impact on the class and helped to embed the ideas in students' minds. The lesson laid a range of foundations for Citizenship. As a new Year 7 class, they had another three years to formalise their understanding of the Citizenship themes within the lesson. As more sessions were programmed in which students could build on these experiences, the impact of this lesson provided an initial exploration of some of the issues that would be addressed later both in Science and other subjects.

These ideas would benefit from some swift reinforcement and the opportunity to discover more about some of the knowledge base of Citizenship. The provision of some background material on the role of taxation either through Science or through links to Citizenship lessons would have helped students to broaden their understanding.

Group work across the curriculum

Business Studies

Mini-enterprise activities develop understanding of how business works and the skills required for contributing to a group.

English

Group work is a key element of the English curriculum and therefore provides many opportunities for the development of Citizenship skills and understanding. Group discussion on a topical issue based on conflicting newspaper reports will allow students to develop an understanding of how the media influences opinion.

Geography

Group exploration of the local area in Year 7 develops an understanding of the local community. Groups can choose different aspects to explore and then share findings.

History

Groups could be asked to research the social, cultural, religious or ethnic diversity of a society they are studying and share their findings with the rest of the class.

ICT

Groups can research a topic on selected sites on the Internet and prepare materials using different software packages including newspapers, leaflets or presentations using PowerPoint or Publisher. This activity can also be used to discuss the power of the media as well as comparing the strengths of different software packages for different uses.

Mathematics

Groups of students can explore geometry using different examples of Islamic art. They might be asked to compare the geometry of their example with the work of a modern European or American artist.

PE

Identify the roles and responsibilities of individuals within a group when planning strategies.

RE

Group project on an individual whose life was centred around a religious vocation helps to develop an understanding of diversity.

Science

Find out about different types of nuclear wastes from UK power stations, how they are presently stored and the prospects for long-term disposal.

Start with a collection of relevant books or simply enter the phrase 'UK nuclear legacy' into an Internet search engine. NIREX http://www.nirex.co.uk/iabout.htm is a useful starting point for this activity.

Questions for reflection

- Come up with three examples of using group work for:
  - brainstorming and discussion
  - solving problems
  - making things.

- When should you intervene in group work? Explain why.
- How can group work help students to develop Citizenship skills within the context of your subject?
- How do other teachers use group work in their subjects?

Chapter 8

Thoughtful presentations

Why use presentations?

When young people carry out Citizenship activities, they frequently need to make presentations to a variety of audiences both in and out of school. They often claim to be too nervous to make such public appearances but practice and careful consideration of the purpose and process of presentations can lead to confident, thoughtful outcomes.

The Citizenship Programme of Study at Key Stage 3 asks students to 'justify orally and in writing a personal opinion about such issues, problems or events'.

At Key Stage 4 they should also justify and defend their point of view. Presentations provide excellent opportunities to demonstrate structured thinking about issues, problems or events. In order to put a presentation together, students will need to 'think about topical political, spiritual, moral, social and cultural issues, problems and events by analysing information and its sources, including ICT based sources'.

Key Stage 4 students should also be researching the issues as well as 'showing an awareness of the use and abuse of statistics'.

Presentations may be informative, persuasive or both. Evidence or research therefore makes an important contribution to any presentation. An informative presentation just needs evidence but a persuasive presentation needs both evidence and thoughtful consideration of the right strategy to persuade a particular audience.

Not only does working on persuasive presentations help students to organise their ideas, but also it helps them to recognise how others influence opinion. Developing an understanding of how the media, political parties, pressure groups, businesses and other organisations set about persuasion will help students to identify and evaluate perspectives.

Presentations often involve responding to questions so students have to develop skills of argument and debate in order to support their points of view. This means that the rationale behind the argument needs to be understood and clearly constructed. Critical thinking therefore plays a key role in the development of presentation skills.

Confidence is a great asset for any young person when participating as a citizen. Presentation skills can be built gently through Key Stages 3 and 4 until approaching people on any issue is no longer daunting. Knowing that the preparation has been done and the arguments practised provides anyone with a sense of security when dealing with others. This will not only benefit their Citizenship development but also add value to all their educational experience.

When students make presentations, others form the audience. This is a learning opportunity in its own right. People are often unwilling to listening to others' points of view when they contradict their own. At Key Stage 4 students are expected to 'be able to think about, express, explain and critically evaluate views that are not their own'.

Listening is clearly essential to developing this skill. As the audience, listening to others' presentations, students are expected to be active participants in order to question effectively. Questioning others constructively develops skills of perception and critical thinking because students have to grasp the points being made, identify flaws in the argument and construct a challenge.

Running presentations

Students are increasingly asked to present their work to the class. The activity might range from reporting back on group work to full-scale presentations resulting from an investigation or other longer piece of work.

Presentations can take a range of forms. They can be based on posters, artefacts, overhead transparencies (OHTs) or presentation software. In Chapter 3 the case study on discussion involved presentations in which the students produced posters composed of graphs and commentary in a Mathematics lesson. This had the advantages of producing interesting display material for the classroom and not being dependent on the use of an ICT room.

Presentations using ICT often help students who lack confidence in their ability to produce work that looks good. It also means that everyone can see the presentation clearly. Posters and other such material can be hard to read from a distance. The students in the case study in Chapter 10 learn Citizenship through ICT lessons and constantly present their work to the rest of the class. They quickly develop confidence and enhanced self-esteem because of the high quality appearance of their presentations.

Although students need to be in an ICT room to create electronic presentations, preparatory work can be carried out in an ordinary classroom. In fact, working initially without a computer can focus minds effectively on the content of the presentation. A laptop computer and a projector work well for the lesson in which the students make their presentations. As wireless networks become more common, the computers can be taken to the students rather than the other way round.

Setting a specific length of time for a presentation is a good discipline for students as it focuses the mind on what has to be said. It also assists classroom organisation because the lesson in which the presentations take place can become rather repetitive, particularly if students are working on the same topic. Planning for questioning has two effects. It makes all students think about everyone else's presentation as well as working out what's likely to be asked of them. Allowing time for groups to work out some questions between each presentation helps develop critical thinking and keeps the whole class involved.

The audience plays a very important part in presentations. Whether it is the class, others within the school or outsiders, an audience influences the attitude of presenters. Young people may suggest that they are nervous when confronted with an audience of outsiders but it often has a powerful effect on their self-esteem because they realise that others are interested in their ideas. Plenty of practice in presenting on a smaller scale will build confidence in preparation for higher profile activities. In Chapter 5 students who had investigated the development of a local leisure facility made their presentations in the town's council chamber to a group including local councillors.

Although they expressed anxiety, they performed well and benefited greatly from the experience.

Learning with presentations

Presentations have a range of beneficial effects on students' learning including the development of communication skills, enhanced critical thinking and raised self-esteem. These all have relevance to Citizenship because they provide students with the skills needed to participate effectively and challenge other people's thinking. Creating and delivering presentations are useful learning tools for both the development of knowledge and understanding as well as elements of participation within the Citizenship Programme of Study.

Communication

By developing and carrying out presentations, students learn to work with both written and oral communications. Many students start by writing everything down and reading it out. With practice, they move away from this to the use of key words, which an audience can remember, and learn to talk with greater confidence.

Being able to distinguish between and use informative and persuasive language is an asset in many circumstances. Presentations provide the opportunity to develop both aspects of communication. As the Citizenship curriculum suggests, the informative skills come first. As students progress into Key Stage 4, they are expected to develop more critical and evaluative communication skills in order to 'express, justify and defend a personal opinion'.

The use of visual material in presentations also develops communication skills. A group of students producing information leaflets on asylum seekers were asked to illustrate them with photographs. They soon realised that the images they selected changed the tone of the leaflet. A picture of children with scared faces pressed against a bus window said more than many words. This opened up a discussion on how pictures can influence people and the realisation that a more threatening image would have a very different impact on readers.

Critical thinking

Creating an effective presentation involves critical thinking because students have to work out exactly how to structure an argument and communicate it to others. Whether the material has been provided for or researched by the students, they have to sort out what is relevant and sequence it to build a case. They can be helped in a variety of ways.

- Define the scope of the presentation.
- Set a limit to the number of screens if using a software package.
- Have time to brainstorm.
- Create a plan.
- Provide writing frames to guide the structure and content.
- Have time to develop and ask questions.

Year 10 students at Ridgeway School in Wroughton, Wiltshire, chose to teach a Year 9 Citizenship class on politics as their General Certificate of Secondary Education (GCSE) Citizenship studies activity. The lesson was a great success and made a strong piece of coursework. As part of it, they made a presentation about the working of the House of Commons which not only provided the class with the necessary information but also made the examination candidates think very hard about the important ideas on the parliamentary system and how to communicate it to best effect. The process involved some significant critical thinking about both aspects of the lesson and contributed to the Citizenship knowledge and skills of both teachers and taught.

Self-esteem

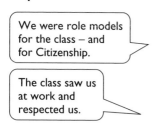

We were role models for the class – and for Citizenship.

The class saw us at work and respected us.

The politics lesson at Ridgeway School gave the Year 10 students a strong sense of self-esteem and the Year 9 students realised what could be achieved by their peers. GCSE Citizenship studies is taken at the end of Year 10 by students who opt for extra lessons to top up the standard curriculum time. Several members of the Year 9 class opted into the course when they reached Year 10.

Gaining self-esteem helps young people to develop as individuals and feel more confident in their ability to achieve. Maslow (1987) argued that people have a hierarchy of needs starting with the basic requirements for food and housing, then rising to higher levels which determine the extent of motivation. Esteem comes high on the list and means that people have a need for achievement, competence, mastery as well as status and prestige. The students at Ridgeway School gained all these when they had taught their lesson. They felt good about themselves.

Working on and presenting the outcomes of their activities provides an opportunity to develop self-esteem and therefore increase motivation. Creating a positive experience means structuring and responding to students' work in ways that help them to achieve positive outcomes.

An individual's self-worth reflects the responses received in the past. The key players in developing self-esteem through presentations are the teacher, peers and any external audience.

- The teacher needs to set the framework, as discussed earlier, so students can research, organise and present their work effectively. As time passes and confidence grows, students will need less direction and support but, initially, they need considerable structure and guidance.
- Classmates are the audience and interrogators. They might be tempted to ridicule others but the realisation that they will have to make their own presentation often overcomes this desire. If everyone has prepared for potential questions, members of the audience can develop confidence in quizzing the speakers and the latter can gain self-esteem by responding effectively.
- Outside audiences are generally very supportive as many are pleasantly surprised at the quality of students' presentations. They are also impressed by the knowledge and interest that students show in something they know a lot about. Briefing outsiders before the event is important, especially if they are judging the groups.

There is a fine line between giving constructive criticism and criticising. The former means that students go away feeling good about themselves and knowing how to do even better next time. Criticism often does the reverse. Self-esteem alone is not enough because it can lead to self-satisfaction without achievement. The students at Ridgeway School demonstrated mastery orientation (Dweck and Leggett 1988) because they were motivated to learn, determined to put together an effective presentation and an active lesson which the Year 9 class would enjoy and learn from.

> **Mastery orientation** refers to a sense of self-competence or self-efficacy that children develop from an early age and that moulds their approach to learning. It is an attitude of: 'I am good at tasks and know how to do them.' Children who are mastery oriented are curious, they want to learn and have developed the resilience to cope with failure and frustration.
>
> (Fisher 1995)

Whatever style of presentation is being carried out, students are often surprised by their own achievement. An initial nervousness is a common reaction so successful outcomes are welcomed by everyone as they help to develop both mastery orientation and self-esteem.

Case study: Citizenship in KS4 Business

The school

Leasowes is an 11–16 comprehensive school in Halesowen, West Midlands. The school has a creative approach to the curriculum with every Friday reserved for extended learning projects. Different subjects can run themed sessions on their own or with other subjects from 8.30 a.m. until 1.30 p.m. The later part of the day can be used for department business or for staff development. Cross-curricular Citizenship not only is supported within some ordinary subject programmes but also underwrites some of the Friday activities.

In Years 10 and 11, the Business department uses some Fridays for completing coursework and also for a variety of investigations with two or three class groups brought together in a large workspace. The department uses networked computers and a set of wireless laptops within the classroom.

In this case study, a group of Year 10 pupils explore the responsibilities of a variety of stakeholders in a community and prepare to make presentations at a planning inquiry.

The lesson

Commentary

Aims

- To identify the ways in which views of stakeholders in a business may co-incide or conflict.
- To develop an initial understanding of how a business works.
- To present a case to a forum of fellow pupils and to ask and answer pertinent questions.
- To understand the ways in which decisions are made in a formal inquiry.

Students have spent a term exploring the workings of different kinds of businesses but have not looked at the impact of businesses and communities on each other.

They are used to preparing reports for their own coursework folders. This exercise is designed to encourage communication between groups and to involve persuasive writing and talking.

Background and content

The normal diet of two-hour lessons is supplemented by this extended day. The class teachers work together to prepare and manage the tasks. Students are given a brief about a sports stadium development and asked to create their own detailed roles within clusters of stakeholder groups. They will spend half the session preparing their views while under pressure from breaking news. The second half will focus on a planning inquiry.

Students will be looking at the views of fans, a local sports council, and local businesses who all stand to gain from the development of a moderately successful football club into an all-purpose sports stadium with national prestige. Local residents, other businesses and environmentalists have other views. The key to this activity is to have sufficient detail for students to involve themselves yet not so much that it swamps them.

The starter

Students are given an overall introduction using a briefing sheet and then divided into groups of six with a particular stakeholder brief. They have a map of the area showing the location of the old ground and the proposed stadium. They are given a very up-beat report from the local paper. They have to create a personal mini-biography, a group name and logo and send an email of their ideas about the development to the local newspaper. (30 minutes)

Students have a mix of given and self-created information to work with. The teachers circulate to make sure they are on task and prompt them to think about the impact of the development using the map and some key questions:

- How far are you from the stadium?
- Will it affect your livelihood or way of life?

- Do you all agree on the pros and cons of the development?
- Is there any information you need to find out?
- Do other groups feel the same way about the development?

The 'emails' are pasted to a shared area on the network so that they are accessible to a teacher who can edit them and circulate if appropriate.

The core: preparation for the presentation

Students work in small groups and respond to a variety of 'newsflashes and reports'. Some of these are pre-prepared; others are drawn from the emails sent by groups.

Some stakeholder groups meet to share ideas and views.

Some groups decide to research information about other stadium developments.

One teacher 'interviews' students for a local TV station using a digital video-recorder.

Groups produce supporting posters and individuals generate notes to be used for their presentations at a later point.

'Expert' briefing sheets are available to help where necessary. (60 minutes)

The regular newsflashes are projected for the whole class to see but without comment from the teachers. Printed reports are circulated from the 'newspaper editor' which carry summaries of different stakeholder views.

Students are left to judge the importance and relevance of these issues for themselves. There is an opportunity here for groups to identify whether they are part of a 'majority' or 'minority' in the support of the development.

They need to make judgements about the key issues which they need to take to the planning inquiry. Some of the newsflashes are very much business-orientated: others involve broad issues for the whole community such as whether a redevelopment should involve people usually considered as 'outsiders'.

Presentations

After a short break, students are given a briefing about the inquiry. They have a writing frame which helps them prepare summaries of their case. They paste these to a shared area and they are used as a projected backdrop for their 5-minute

The writing frame directs students to five key points for the main substance of their presentation. It also suggests they anticipate three or four questions which they might be asked by others and consider questions they might themselves ask.

presentation to the inquiry. Each group has a presenter and an 'expert witness' to provide back-up information if needed. Other groups can cross-question after the presentations.

A teacher acts as chief planning inspector and is supported by two students in similar roles.

After all the presentations, all students register their views by a quick vote. The inspectors retire to make a decision while the groups evaluate their own presentations and success in the whole venture. (60 minutes)

The inquiry rules provide a tight deadline and each group knows it has one chance to make a major impact on the inquiry.

The teacher as planning inspector can call for an adjournment – or 'time out' – if a major issue comes up unexpectedly or if groups need more time to consider a key question. The teacher can also ask questions in role if students have missed important issues.

The back projection of each group's key issues allows everyone to take notice of all five points and provides groups with the option to add any additional publicity materials such as images or data downloaded from the web as part of their research.

This information is available on the shared space on the network for a later review by all groups if necessary.

Plenary

A teacher briefly outlines the way in which real-life inquiries operate. The emphasis is on the 'right to be heard' and the relative weight given to carefully researched cases. (10 minutes)

The teacher and students acting as planning inspectors report on their verdict. Students review their ideas of 'success'. A short class discussion focuses on the ways of making a case to such an inquiry and on which groups seemed to have the most success. (10 minutes)

Finally, the teacher asks students to complete an evaluation sheet which underscores the meaning of stakeholders, their importance to the development of the business and the community, and the importance of understanding the process of presenting a case to a public forum. (10 minutes)

Students in the majority at the inquiry were convinced the day was theirs and received a shock when the inspectors turned down the development at this point for lack of convincing supporting argument.

There was a discussion about the difference between persuasive and informative language. The inspectors said the local council and other businesses, for example, were making wild claims about the development on the basis of 'ifs' and 'maybes'.

An environmental group had researched the different ways in which a badger colony could be managed in the face of such developments. They were delighted that their work had carried some weight.

The alliance made between the local council and the sports development board was an effective strategy for sharing presentations. Some students admitted to being uneasy because the council should be speaking for everyone, including elderly people, who might not use such a stadium. Business students were left to think about:

- whether stakeholders usually agree or disagree
- whether it is a good idea to join together with others before an important meeting
- what makes a good presentation when there is both an audience and special inspectors to convince
- the importance of their 'right to be heard' as a principle of good Citizenship.

The starter: stakeholder views

After the upbeat presentation which introduced the activity, the students set about working on the views of their stakeholder group. Each group had been given a briefing sheet and an article from the local paper.

ALL FUN AND GAMES FOR THE TOWN OF VALE!

After months of speculation and rumour, proposals have finally been unveiled for the new grounds for Vale Harriers Football Club. The local Sports Council revealed its plans in a press conference yesterday and it looks like the club are destined for a complete change of scene. The plans show a high-tech, all inclusive Sports Stadium which will not only be used by the football team, but is set to become a national venue for both sport and entertainment. The all-seated 80,000 capacity stadium offers something for everyone! Its sport and leisure facilities include a retractable roof, under-soil heating, an indoor arena and entertainment village. Attractions include lots of shopping, bars and restaurants, a multi-screen cinema, bowling alley, ice-rink and a range of creche facilities. The complex is likely to become a huge national attraction, with pop concerts, sports events and full leisure and recreation facilities for all ages! The stadium is set to bring huge benefits to both community and business in the surrounding areas. Local residents should never be bored again, with one of the country's top entertainment complexes right on their doorstep!

Group briefing sheet

Stakeholder Activity: OTHER BUSINESSES

You are a group of local business owners whose businesses such as a fish & chip shop and taxi firm are near to the old Vale Harriers Football Club based in the town centre of Vale.

A move to the new sports stadium, in Little Vale, could mean a 20% loss in profit. Many customers who use your businesses, when the old Vale Harriers Football Club is in use, will spend their money at the businesses, such as fish & chips shops and taxi firms, that are nearer, or located in, the new sports stadium as these will be more convenient for them to use before, during or after a match or event.

You have to formulate an argument to take to the planning meeting. Also, think about counter-arguments.

Other stakeholder groups are:

- The Sports Council   Builders
- Fans of Vale Harriers FC   Eco-Warriors
- The Council   Shareholders
- Local residents near to the new site

A group at work: stakeholders representing other Vale businesses

The group took a positive approach to the change as shown by the following quotes from the businesses that they chose.

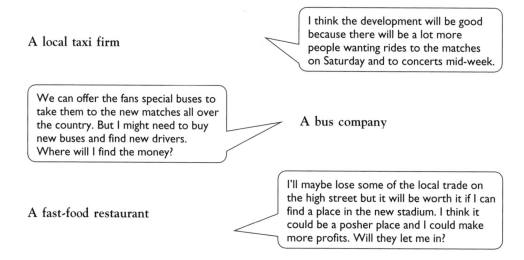

A local taxi firm

> I think the development will be good because there will be a lot more people wanting rides to the matches on Saturday and to concerts mid-week.

> We can offer the fans special buses to take them to the new matches all over the country. But I might need to buy new buses and find new drivers. Where will I find the money?

A bus company

A fast-food restaurant

> I'll maybe lose some of the local trade on the high street but it will be worth it if I can find a place in the new stadium. I think it could be a posher place and I could make more profits. Will they let me in?

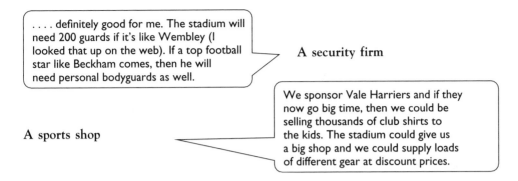

... . definitely good for me. The stadium will need 200 guards if it's like Wembley (I looked that up on the web). If a top football star like Beckham comes, then he will need personal bodyguards as well.

A security firm

A sports shop

We sponsor Vale Harriers and if they now go big time, then we could be selling thousands of club shirts to the kids. The stadium could give us a big shop and we could supply loads of different gear at discount prices.

Core: preparing for the presentation

The 'Other Vale Business' group came to the following conclusions.

Our five main points are:

- more jobs for local people (500+) through our businesses
- profits for lots of different people (us and shareholders and workers)
- more roads and safety features for the new stadium (takes it away from the small estate where the ground is at present)
- most people are in favour of it
- will bring tourism and customers to Vale.

We might be asked about

- Could the stadium go elsewhere?
- Yes, but it would then be too far from town and the motorway and the traffic might have to cross town.

Are we being greedy about profits?

No; everyone needs profits – it's how you survive and everyone will get a kind of share anyway.

Will there be transport problems?

Yes, but it will be needed anyway, we can help with traffic measures like traffic lights together with the council, and our security guards could help with safety before and after matches.

Making the presentations

Views of different stakeholder groups made through presentations.

Local council

The group chose to make a joint presentation with the Stadium shareholders.
The council made several points:

- more jobs
- a better local infrastructure
- put the city on the map
- spin-off for schools
- a big feel-good factor.

The shareholders added some more:

- more money for the club
- attraction of star players
- a short-term cost as tax for longer term benefits.

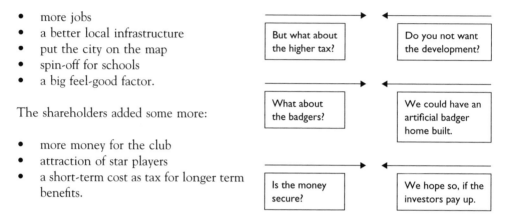

Figure 8.1

Local residents

The presentation was made in front of a backdrop of their questions but also images of dead badgers, heavy lorries, children's learning comes first.

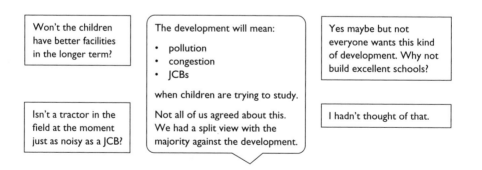

Figure 8.2

Reflection

The teachers were pleased with the ways in which different groups took on the responsibility for presenting their case.

> I was very impressed with the students' attitudes. They took it all so seriously.

> I thought I was going to have to help the groups but they managed their own time and the information very well.

There were lively exchanges between some groups as they tried to harness support for their case before the Inquiry.

> Some of the students said I was misbehaving in my role as journalist. They've never said boo to a goose before!

> There were some students who led presentations who have not taken much part in my other lessons.

There was a real tension at the moment of presenting each case and several groups had worked hard on the 'extras' that might tilt the decisions their way. One group chose an emotional poster as backdrop, another group chose their drama specialist to make their presentation, a third used humour and heckling to challenge other presenters.

Some groups have more of a challenge on their hands so there is scope for differentiation. It is worth guiding higher attaining students towards representing the council, for example, rather than the environmentalists.

> The council group found their task quite hard. The environmentalists had an easier job in many ways.

Although the students had been given a briefing on the rules of the inquiry, it came as a surprise to many that the stadium development was rejected because the presentations were short of supporting evidence. This may be a good strategy to challenge students' assumptions, but many felt let down because the 'rules had changed'. This would be made much clearer from the outset if the groups had been given a selection of key information from which they could choose to supplement their own research.

> I think this is a good example of a way to mix the best of Business with a real Citizenship issue.

Overall the teachers were happy with the activity. It drew out a range of issues which the two subjects have in common as well as the skills which add value to any subject and help to develop young people's ability to play an effective role in the community.

Developing Citizenship understanding

Business studies provides many opportunities to develop Citizenship knowledge and skills. It covers a range of topics that many teachers find hard to deal with, such as the need for an understanding of the interrelationships within the economy. The Citizenship Programme of Study asks students to know 'how the economy functions, including the role of business and financial services'.

Even at a simple level, a teacher needs to appreciate the links between taxation and government spending and the trade-offs which governments face when making decisions. On the business front, the subject provides a clear understanding of how resources are combined to make a product and earn a profit, provided the organisation is run effectively.

The activity in the case study is primarily about stakeholders but is in the context of business and the economy. Stakeholders are a very useful way of looking at any issue because it helps students to see the world from different perspectives and look at ways of resolving conflict.

Other issues which crop up include local democracy as one group of students represent the local council and therefore the local population. The local environment is also represented as is the media.

The response to the question 'But what about the higher taxes?' showed that students had clearly picked up the relationship between taxation and spending and the trade-offs in decision-making. By saying 'But do you want the development?' the students demonstrated the link had been made. The trade-offs were also shown by one group's suggestion that better schools should be built instead of the sports complex.

Environmental issues are clearly represented as the students had identified the need for an artificial badger set.

Developing Citizenship skills

The activity asks students to build a reasoned argument from a particular perspective. As this perspective might not be one supported by the individual, they had to 'use their imagination to consider other people's experiences and be able to think about, express, explain and critically evaluate views that are not their own'.

The evaluation took place because they had to work out the questions that might be asked and respond to those that were asked.

In putting together the presentation, they had to 'express, justify and defend orally and in writing a personal opinion about such issues, problems or events'.

Many used a mix of words and images to get their message over. The selection of images that ran behind each presentation showed that they were putting into practice the persuasive skills they learn from the media.

At all stages they were 'contributing to group and exploratory class discussions' as they had to work together to develop a stance and then build the presentation as effectively as they could.

Enhancing Citizenship

Developing a leisure centre is an integral part of a Citizenship programme as well as being a good context for learning Business studies. It therefore readily combines the two subjects. QCA's schemes of work include a similar activity. Each student's outcomes can therefore be gathered together to contribute to their Citizenship Portfolio. Adding a final task sheet that draws clearly from the Citizenship Programme of Study and makes the links would help to embed the ideas firmly as making a contribution to both subjects.

The activity itself could readily be used in discrete Citizenship lessons because everything that is addressed is included in the Programme of Study. A topical local question would be particularly appropriate as familiarity often stirs added interest in students. Seeking support from a Business or Economics teacher would also assist in making the links and connections necessary to develop ideas fully.

Presentations across the curriculum

Business Studies

Students work in groups to explore and present information about how different businesses approach social responsibility.

Design and Technology

A presentation on the environmental impact of a product and its assessment for sustainability. Students should be asked to consider how the impact could be minimised.

English

Many texts that students read include aspects that fit into the Citizenship Programme of Study. Groups of students can make presentations on these aspects and comparisons can be drawn between them.

History

A presentation related to the post-1900 world study. A focus on the need for mutual respect and understanding offers much potential.

ICT

Find out about local MPs, their roles and any issues in which they have been involved. Most MPs have their own websites and further information is available on the Explore Parliament and *Guardian* websites. The information can be gathered into a PowerPoint presentation.

Mathematics

Students create a short presentation aimed at helping other members of the class to understand a particular topic by putting it into a context. Data handling might use a variety of graphs to show information about aspects of their local community. Use percentages, fractions and decimals to show evidence of changes taking place in the UK population.

MFL

Students can work in groups to create presentations on different aspects of a country's culture in order to demonstrate diversity.

PE

In dance, students make presentations showing how their work reflects different social and cultural contexts.

RE

Presentations to support a campaign usually work well. Ask students to put together a campaign and defend their point of view while others prepare to challenge them.

Science

Use the following resource as a basis for student research and presentations on food safety: http://www.sycd.co.uk/only_connect/pdf/everywhere/citizenship/food_safety.pdf.

Questions for reflection

- What topics in my subject, which lend themselves to presentations, share outcomes with Citizenship?
- How can the Citizenship outcomes be highlighted?
- How does the presence of outsiders benefit students making presentations in Citizenship? How can it be organised?

Chapter 9

Learning with simulations

Why use simulations?

Citizenship at KS3 and KS4 asks young people to consider multidimensional issues that relate to a range of curriculum areas. Using simulations is an effective and engaging strategy for developing an understanding of how different aspects of an issue interact. They are available in a range of subjects and many are appropriate for use in Citizenship. Whether paper or ICT-based the learning models and outcomes work on the same principles.

Examples of multidimensional issues in Citizenship

- The wider issues and challenges of global interdependence and responsibility, including sustainable development and Local Agenda 21.
- How the economy functions, including the role of business and financial services.

Source: QCA Citizenship Programme of Study KS4

In the context of education, a simulation is a recreation of the real world, sometimes in a form designed to elicit particular learning objectives. A school's Citizenship programme will be full of situations that students cannot encounter first hand, so a good simulation, whether ICT-based or not, can create a valuable learning experience.

Most simulations are set up for students to make choices on the basis of a range of information. The outcome of their choices becomes apparent and students learn from the consequences of the decisions. As a result they develop an understanding of the concepts and skills associated with the area of study. The approach facilitates the development of deeper rather than superficial learning. In *President for a Day*, for example, students develop an understanding of the complexity of issues facing a developing country. A simulation about the local council's decision-making will ask students to come to conclusions about the trade-offs involved in drawing up the budget.

The nature of simulations means that they appeal to a range of different learning styles because they often use a variety of materials and tasks that combine words, images and opportunities to contribute in different ways. When students work together on a simulation, their mix of learning styles can enhance the outcomes for others. This also helps them to appreciate the value of participating in a group.

There are particular features which make simulations an attractive teaching method for developing Citizenship skills. When the simulation is in the context of another subject it is useful to identify these skills and make them explicit in the lesson's objectives.

No right answer

Real life is complex and answers to problems are rarely simple. Students need to learn that there are many alternatives and that 'it depends' is often a good answer – not an evasive one.

Simulations often allow students to see the impact of different strategies from the decisions that they take. Many have built-in 'shocks' which demonstrate how there is no right answer to a problem because the future brings uncertainty. Citizens are always facing uncertainty so this is a valuable learning experience.

Have a go

Simulations also give students the opportunity to have a go. They are not dependent on the wisdom of others but are asked to work on or develop their knowledge and understanding in order to come to conclusions for themselves.

Most simulations provide opportunities to have more than one go, so students can use trial and error to watch the changes that take place as a result of their actions. As students progress through each round, they begin to recognise the assumptions built into the simulation and their decisions become more sophisticated.

Simulations are therefore an effective way of using the learning model of doing, reviewing, learning and applying. In many simulations, whether ICT-based or not, this learning cycle is built into the process.

Developing perspectives

In order to respond to the questions raised by simulations, students need to be able to appreciate a range of perspectives on an issue. Whether decisions are about how the government spends its money or whether a developing country should borrow or not, the ability to see things from a variety of points of view is clearly important.

Most simulations involve choices that represent different viewpoints. Students can discuss a decision and record it as well as their reasons for the choice.

Using simulations

ICT-based simulations are often designed for one student, sitting in front of a computer, to work through the stages. In Citizenship and much of the rest of the curriculum, this does not necessarily lead to the desired learning outcomes. It is therefore important to ensure that lessons are planned carefully to build in interaction and opportunities for discussion.

The case study in this chapter shows how students became much more involved with the process when they had to discuss and justify their decisions.

There are some simple rules to follow in running a simulation.

The starter

The starter is an introduction that draws out the purpose of the activity, provides an overview and clarifies any concepts that need to be used. This may reinforce prior learning if the aim of the lesson is to practise its application. It may also form an introduction to a topic if the simulation is a first encounter with part of the course. If the simulation is taking place in another curriculum subject but is being used to develop Citizenship understanding and skills, it may be important to plant ideas about this broader relevance.

Orientation

Any simulation requires a little practice to be able to work it effectively. Some programmes include a practice run that allows students to find out how things work. If this is not the case, they will need a guidance sheet to follow and prompt them at moments of uncertainty. Many simulations take longer than one lesson and it may be wise to carry out these two initial stages in the previous lesson. If so, a short, sharp starter should reinforce the objectives and processes of the activity in the lesson in which the simulation takes place.

The simulation

While the students work on the simulation, they will need support and guidance when required. Different parts of a simulation may need different approaches. Some tasks may be best done alone, in pairs or as a group. Computer based simulations are often set up as individual activities but higher quality learning often takes place when students are encouraged to work together. If the activity involves various stages, it may be appropriate to stop at the end of Stage 1 in order to exchange outcomes, perspectives and ideas.

The case study in this chapter shows how a teacher used one computer and a projector in the classroom and worked towards a democratic decision, made by the class as a whole, at each stage of the simulation. The structure of the lesson led to the development of understanding of the democratic process as well as a willingness to participate and listen to other people's points of view.

Whatever strategy is used, the work should be collaborative rather than isolated. This will encourage social learning and help students to appreciate different perspectives.

The plenary

The debriefing pulls together the outcomes of the simulation and reinforces the learning that has taken place. It will help the class to analyse and draw conclusions. As simulations are always a step away from real life, it is also worth considering the ways in which it is both realistic and unrealistic in its assumptions.

When used in the context of Citizenship, the activity and the plenary need to draw out both the subject-based conclusions and the relevance of the activity to young people's role as citizens. This is where the Citizenship co-ordinator can play an important role along-side the subject teacher. Even when the activity is clearly in the Programme of Study, the interpretation is often different when looked at from the Citizenship perspective and will require a different set of review questions.

Learning with simulations

The strategy involved in learning with simulations lends itself to Citizenship. Students develop a strong grasp of cause and consequence as a result of seeing the impact of their decisions. The realisation that their own decisions and activities have consequences in a wide range of contexts should be an integral part of any Citizenship programme.

Many simulations meet QCA's Citizenship Programme of Study requirement to 'think about topical political, spiritual, moral, social and cultural issues, problems and events by analysing information and its sources, including ICT-based resources'.

Working through a simulation also gives students a sense of their own worth as learners. They are not dependent on being told. They are making their own decisions and learning from them. This increases confidence in their own abilities to develop understanding, analyse and draw conclusions. This comes from an appreciation of the cause-and-effect relationship and a sensitivity to feedback from their peers, teachers and any guidance in the simulation.

ICT-based simulations often prove motivating for students. They find them fun to use and learning is enhanced as a result. Some students, however, struggle with the number of variables that need to be considered when decisions are required, so it may be important

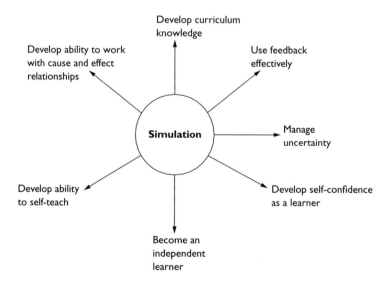

Figure 9.1

to organise groups in which there is a balance of ability. Simulations that have recognis-
able stages are generally easier to manage. The provision of information on a 'need to
know' basis is generally more effective than swamping students with material at an early
stage.

Most simulations have built-in chance cards that may improve the situation or make
it worse. The learning that results from making decisions in these changing situations
is powerful in the Citizenship context. In many subjects, young people are taught that
there is a right and wrong answer but in Citizenship this is often not the case. There may
be 659 MPs in the House of Commons but real Citizenship comes from the ability
to weigh up situations in which a variety of stakeholders have a range of perspectives
(see Figure 9.1).

Case study: Citizenship in KS3 Geography

The school

South Dartmoor Community College is in Ashburton, on the southern slopes of Dartmoor. It is a popular comprehensive school with 1,600 students across the full ability
range. It draws students from the small town of Ashburton and the surrounding villages of
Dartmoor.

The school runs a cross-curricular Citizenship programme. Subject teachers are asked
to audit their schemes of work for opportunities to fulfil the Programme of Study. The
co-ordinator monitors the proposals in order to develop a programme for the school as a
whole. The teachers were involved in an in-service training (INSET) session, led by the
co-ordinator, to prepare for the introduction of the subject. Further INSET and dissemina-
tion of information has been delivered to heads of department at management and
curriculum team meetings and passed on to staff at department meetings.

President for a Day was undertaken in a Year 9 Geography class following the National
Curriculum.

The lesson	Commentary
Aims	
• To draw together and apply learning on development issues. • To develop the concept of voting. • To develop discussion skills.	The school runs cross-curricular Citizenship and meets the requirements for global interdependence through Geography at KS3 and 4. There is a good fit between the two subjects on this topic and it offers opportunities to develop Citizenship skills.

Background and content

The basis for the lesson is *President for a Day*, a computer simulation produced by the Tear Fund (2001). It shows trade-offs in a range of development decisions. The students take on the role of president of a less economically developed country (LEDC) and have to make decisions in light of information provided by several 'experts'.

President for a Day builds on prior understanding from Geography in this context. It could also be used in situations where less background knowledge is available but discussion might be more anecdotal.

It portrays the problems faced by such countries clearly and helps students to appreciate that the issues are complex and that there is no easy solution.

The starter

The teacher introduced the lesson with a quick question-and-answer session to refresh memories about earlier work on development.

The activity takes about an hour so the introduction needed to be quick, or carried out in the previous lesson.

The core

Students watched the introductory part of the ICT-based simulation as a whole class and worked in pairs each time a decision was to be made. They then voted on what should be done. The whole class then discussed the decision and voted again to see if the discussion had changed people's views.

Each stage of the activity combined geographical knowledge and understanding with a growing facility with skills of debate, discussion and an appreciation of the democratic process. Students contributed willingly because they had rehearsed their arguments with a partner. They were required to justify their point of view and not just make a statement. The decision changed on several occasions as students listened to each other's points of view.

The plenary

The lesson finished with a review of the issues that reinforced knowledge and understanding.

The students had clearly gained from the lesson. Their understanding of the challenges faced by a LEDC was greatly enhanced. They were also willing to participate in this final exchange of ideas.

Resources: President for a Day

Here is a sample of the simulation. There are several rounds with increasingly difficult economic and social problems to be dealt with.

The president is posed a difficult problem

President Mwlagi – we had to borrow money from abroad to rescue us from the situation we were in and to diversify our economy. Since taking out our loan we have managed to keep up with our interest repayments but haven't as yet managed to pay back any capital so we haven't reduced the principal debt.

Some of the material and resources we have been using were given to us on the basis that we would pay for them later. That time has now come and we need to pay our bills but we haven't got the money. Any money our economy has made has been used to cover the interest on the loan.

I fear economic collapse. Commodity prices for the goods we are producing have fallen and we simply aren't making enough money. Our economy is in ruins and we have a budget deficit at home. Interest rates are increasing and so the amount we are paying on the original loan is likely to rise.

What shall we do? Some of your government say we should do nothing because conditions might improve but others say we should borrow more.

Your advisers are waiting to talk to you, President Mwlagi, so please listen to what they have to say. Then it is up to you to decide.

The president is offered advice on this problem by two different advisers.

Adviser 1

President Mwlagi – you can't just keep on borrowing money. We are struggling to meet our interest repayments as it is and these are likely to increase as the interest rates are still rising. We haven't even yet reduced our principle debt, so it would be economic suicide to borrow more. The situation would only get worse.

I advise that we halt all development. Our people will just have to accept that we just can't do all that we promised because of circumstances outside our control. Our economy comes first and we should do all in our power to reduce our loan before we borrow any more money.

The advice is summed up on the screen (Figure 9.2a).

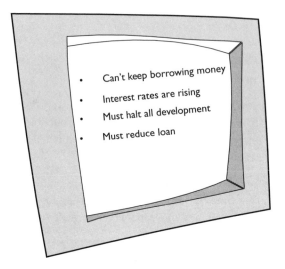

- Can't keep borrowing money
- Interest rates are rising
- Must halt all development
- Must reduce loan

Figure 9.2a

Adviser 2

President Mwlagi – you must take action. We have come so far with our economy we can't see all our hard work go to waste. Remember the strong and independent country we are all longing for. We want to be a great and modern nation and this is what our people dream of. Let us not disappoint them.

If we have not got enough money we must borrow more, then we will be able to complete our development so that we are in a strong position to pay back the money. The West is happy to continue lending to us so why not take advantage of a helping hand?

Have confidence, President Mwlagi, in our people and our country. It makes sense to complete what we have set out to do. Let's not give up now. Let's finish our development. We just need to borrow a bit more. It makes sense.

On the screen (Figure 9.2b).

Figure 9.2b

The students are given the option (Figure 9.2c).

Figure 9.2c

Review

The students enjoyed the lesson because they were put in the driving seat. They felt that the simulation helped their understanding by providing a range of perspectives. Many of their comments showed that they appreciated that the decisions made were the result of weighing up the pros and cons of each strategy. Interviews with students following the lesson showed a range of understanding of the issues but all had a clear picture of trade-offs and the complexity of the decisions to be made.

Their understanding of active Citizenship was enhanced as they had participated in democratic decision-making and been involved in influencing each other's decisions.

They also showed how the teaching strategy used had enhanced their learning and helped them to recognise the nature of different approaches.

Figure 9.3

Reflection

President for a Day proved a successful way of engaging young people in a complex area of the Citizenship curriculum. Dealing with issues like the pros and cons of development strategies is not easy for teachers who are not subject specialists, because of the range of background knowledge and understanding that is required to evaluate students' comments and answers. Many resources produced by interest groups portray a one-sided story that is difficult to challenge without a degree of expertise. *President for a Day* does use the Tear Fund's angle to sum up potential outcomes, but it does not permeate the whole activity. A choice can be made about how to use the Tear Fund's conclusions. A class can come to their own conclusions and then be offered the evaluation included in the simulation to compare with their own. Alternatively, the simulation can run to the end when students can evaluate the Tear Fund's conclusions.

Developing Citizenship understanding

The activity clearly contributes to the KS3 programme of study: 'The world as a global community, and the political, economic, environmental and social implications of this'.

It builds an understanding of the interrelationships of all these aspects of running a developing country and some of the connections with the rest of the world. The students' comments show their achievements.

When a student says, 'We didn't want to borrow but we wanted more hospitals', there is a clear appreciation of the dilemma faced by the president and many less developed economies.

Statements like: 'I disagreed with the vote because interest rates were rising and we wouldn't be able to repay' shows the level of understanding that has been developed. The student not only understands what interest rates are but also is evaluating the options.

Geography provides a good vehicle for this part of the Citizenship curriculum as it is integral to the KS3 course. It is important to be sure that students have transferred the understanding of the ideas and concepts into their perception of themselves as citizens. To achieve this, the activity should include debriefing or a further stage which develops the context of the work.

Students might be asked to transfer their thinking to a topic of current concern. A country that has been devastated by a natural disaster or war might be used to give students the opportunity to work out how the ideas can be applied in a real situation. The activity might draw on newspaper articles or web-based news material as well as some geographical information as background sources.

The teacher's lesson plan has been developed to contribute to the understanding of how the electoral system works. Each decision was taken democratically so students had the opportunity to watch themselves and others as voters, to observe how people are persuaded to change their minds – or not. This is a practice that can be incorporated into many different types of activity so students can participate in democracy at work in different circumstances.

Developing Citizenship skills

The simulation and associated lesson has addressed many of the Citizenship skills of inquiry and communication. Students need continuous practice in these skills to develop a way of thinking about issues. Initially many students just want to express a point of view without supporting the argument. As they progress through Citizenship, the appreciation that they must justify their answers should become embedded in their practice. The ability to persuade others of their perspective through rational argument is the final stage of development – one which many adults find difficult to achieve.

Developing skills of inquiry and communication

Thinking about a topical issue and evaluating evidence

 Justify orally a personal opinion about the issue.

 Contribute to group and exploratory class discussions
Source: adapted from QCA Citizenship Programme of Study

Lesson planning has been critical to these students' achievement. They could have simply worked their way through the simulation individually and gained little in the way of inquiry and communication skills.

The teacher has looked carefully at the requirements for both developing understanding and skills and planned a lesson that helps the students achieve both. The integration of discussion in pairs and as a class group was given focus by the votes. The stress on justifying your point of view when making a comment builds an environment in which unsupported argument is not acceptable. Listening to and considering other people's views is an integral part of the process. Students voted after discussion in pairs and then after whole class discussion so they had to listen to the debate and decide whether to stay with their original views or change in the light of argument.

A student who says, 'I could see both sides of the argument', is clearly starting to deal with a range of perspectives and to appreciate that people have other points of view. It is a challenging and sophisticated skill to look at a problem from someone else's point of view.

When a students says, 'I was persuaded by other people's reasoning', the process is under way.

Some students were even beginning to observe the dynamics of persuasion and the ways in which groups of people with similar identities tend to reinforce each other's perspectives: 'When you work in pairs, you're often with a friend – because they sit next to you. Friends often have the same ideas about things.'

These statements and others on previous pages show the start of the process in which students learn to 'use their imagination to consider other people's experiences and be able to think, express and explain views that are not their own.'

This is the first of the skills of participation and responsible action in the Citizenship Programme of Study.

Meeting attainment targets

Building a portfolio of evidence from across the curriculum involves developing tasks which meet the needs of both the curriculum subject and Citizenship if the burden of work is to be kept to a minimum. To achieve this effectively, the Citizenship co-ordinator needs to work closely with subject departments to work out the best approach.

Encouraging students to ask questions about the issue gives guidance to the construction of evidence. The KS3 Citizenship Scheme of Work Review Unit suggests that students should be asking questions like:

- What does this have to do with me?
- Do I have any responsibility?
- Is there anything I can do to influence the situation?

In this context it is important to work out with the Geography teacher how responding to such questions can contribute to the subject. This simulation leads students to appreciate the issues facing the International Monetary Fund when lending money to less economically developed countries (LEDCs).

Not cross-curricular?

In a school where Citizenship is being taught by class tutors, a simulation of this sort can be used by non-specialists with some help from the specialist. It might be necessary to put together a small pack which gives the non-specialist some background and the transfer activity to ensure that the understanding and skills are successfully developed.

It is also worth considering using a carousel approach so that tutors with special areas of expertise rotate through a number of tutor groups. Any year group is likely to have a reasonable spread of subject teachers so the stress of developing and delivering unfamiliar material can be reduced.

Simulations across the curriculum

Business Studies

The Trade Game from Christian Aid demonstrates equity issues related to free trade. There are many mini-enterprise activities which demonstrate how businesses work.

Geography

The Behari Farmer is a CD-based simulation that guides students through the difficulties of farming and maintaining a family in Bihar. It is available from John Stainfield on jdstainfield@aol.com.

History

The BBC history website has some simple simulations in which students make choices. One of them looks at the decisions of a Victorian councillor about improving living conditions in an industrial town: http://www.bbc.co.uk/history/society_culture/.

RE

A range of CDs provide interactive simulations on worship in different religions.

Science

'Sars is coming!' physically models the spread of an infectious disease through the class over one lesson, or the whole school over a few days: http://www.ase.org.uk/htm/ teacher_zone/upd8/upd8_11/upd8_week11_pdfs/zars.pdf with related teaching notes at http://www.ase.org.uk/htm/teacher_zone/upd8/upd8_11/upd8_zars.php.

Questions for reflection

- What advantages do simulations have as a teaching strategy?
- Are there subject-based simulations which have a Citizenship dimension?
- How would the Citizenship issues within a particular simulation be highlighted and reflected upon?

Chapter 10

Informing and communicating with technology

Why ICT and Citizenship?

When schools are deciding how to incorporate Citizenship into the curriculum, the question asked most frequently is 'How do we make the space?' A solution that has been adopted by a number of schools across the United Kingdom is to merge ICT and Citizenship.

It makes a happy marriage because much of the content of the KS3 and KS4 Programme of Study for ICT lends itself to Citizenship. The extract from the KS3 ICT Programme of Study demonstrates how well the two subjects fit together. It offers opportunities to explore and research issues, interpret and evaluate information and present findings effectively – all skills which are required in Citizenship.

Extract from ICT at KS3

Students are taught

- how to obtain information well matched to purpose
- how to collect, enter, analyse and evaluate quantitative and qualitative information
- to develop and explore information, solve problems and derive new information for particular purposes
- how to use ICT to test predictions and discover patterns and relationships
- how to interpret information and to reorganise and present it in a variety of forms that are fit for purpose
- to use a range of ICT tools efficiently to draft, bring together and refine information and create good quality presentations in a form that is sensitive to the needs of particular audiences and suits the information content
- working with a range of information to consider its characteristics, structure, organisation and purposes
- be independent and discriminating when using ICT.

                                    Source: National Curriculum website

---

The active element of a Citizenship course can also be enhanced greatly with opportunities to use ICT to create leaflets, market events, provide information and work out results. If students are expected to keep a log of their activities, ICT provides the natural vehicle.

Students are often delighted at the quality of work produced using ICT because it looks much more professional than the hand-written version. This helps them to have a positive view of their achievement and boosts self-esteem.

The combination of the two subjects is not just a one-way benefit. Citizenship offers a coherent context for ICT lessons which helps students to develop knowledge, skills and understanding. Often ICT teachers look for material from a range of subjects to use as the context for developing students' abilities. This clearly has a value because young people are working with material that is familiar from other subjects. The strength of using Citizenship is that ICT is used with a very clear purpose to assist learning. Students can therefore see the outcomes of their developing ICT skills and understanding in the Citizenship Portfolio.

In the early years of Citizenship it is important to establish the credibility of the subject with both staff and students. A course in e-Citizenship, as one school has called it, assists greatly with this process because teachers can see it clearly on the curriculum and students are following the course in a context they often enjoy. Motivation plays a critical role in any teaching but a new subject often needs a little extra help.

In many schools access to ICT facilities for Citizenship can be a problem because the rooms are booked for other subjects which have established a need. The strategy of combining Citizenship with ICT clearly overcomes this problem.

It is important to make sure that the course meets the requirements of both subjects in content, teaching and learning styles and outcomes. In all cross-curricular contexts the same issue arises, ensuring that students are attaining both the subject specific outcomes as well as the Citizenship outcomes. This will involve the students working co-operatively in their inquiries in ICT lessons. Such strategies will enhance Citizenship learning and skill development. One factor to be borne in mind, however, is that students need careful guidance on the use of the Internet, so it is essential to consult the school's Health and Safety policy before beginning. The topic of Internet safety, in fact, can be used for Citizenship lessons as it deals with rights and responsibilities and the role of the media.

Learning with ICT

ICT lessons are a good venue for working on group activities that require research and yet develop skills. Students can have clearly defined tasks that contribute to a group outcome and have outcomes that are attributable to individuals. They therefore serve the joint purpose of meeting both ICT and Citizenship objectives. For more about working in groups, see Chapter 7.

Often Citizenship works best when authentic documents and information are available. ICT assists this process as the Internet gives instant access to many resources that are not easily available in other ways. It is, for example, often difficult to access a range of different places of worship but the web provides images and information to meet this need. Being able to see real, live places generally has a much greater impact than words and pictures in books.

Mind mapping

The Citizenship Programme of Study asks students to 'think about topical political, spiritual, moral, social and cultural issues, problems and events by analysing information and its sources, including ICT based sources' and 'justify orally and in writing a personal opinion about such issues, problems or events'.

If students are to use evidence, draw conclusions and solve problems, having a structure to work with helps them to organise their ideas. Mind-mapping software provides a vehicle for doing this. It helps them to think laterally rather than in a linear direction and encourages them to realise that there is often no one right answer to a problem.

Mind maps, for example, can be drawn up from different people's perspectives and therefore demonstrate clearly how different people have varying views and how this influences their decisions. ICT again helps students to work in an interesting way that appeals to them.

Developing inductive thinking

ICT provides access to a wealth of information for Citizenship. An exploration of religious identities, for example, might draw on the BBC World Service website which provides a description of the beliefs and activities of all the main religious groups. *Social Trends*, *Regional Trends* and local data on the National Statistics website will help students to discover how many people in the United Kingdom belong to minority ethnic groups, where they live and their point of origin.

Who lives in the United Kingdom?

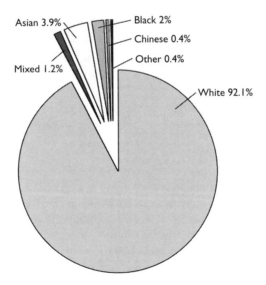

Figure 10.1 UK ethnic groupings
Source: Office for National Statistics, 2001.

Where do they live?

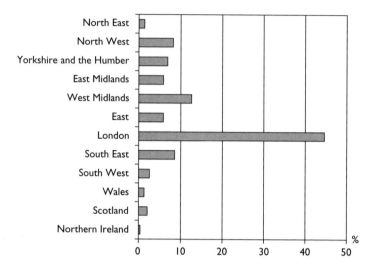

Figure 10.2 Regional distribution of the non-white population
Source: Office for National Statistics, 2001.

The phases of inductive thinking

- Gather and present data that is relevant to a topic or problem.
- Examine and enumerate the data into categories with common attributes.
- Classify the data and develop labels for the categories that can be used as a means of identification.
- Use the categories to develop hypotheses or skills.

Source: adapted from Joyce *et al.* 1997

They can explore their own region and compare it with others and ask questions about why communities differ. Such activities can encourage inductive thinking.

Working through the processes of inductive thinking encourages students to use the data available to develop ideas and draw conclusions. ICT can then offer the opportunities to present the outcomes in ways that add clarity to the thinking processes and purpose. This might result in a leaflet for people in the area showing the variety of cultural inputs into the community.

Solving problems

ICT gives students a degree of independence. A lesson or series of lessons, with clear objectives and good direction, help students to develop their ICT skills while solving a Citizenship problem.

A group of students, working collaboratively, can explore the issue, discuss strategies, make plans, research information, contact organisations, review outcomes, come to a reasoned conclusion and present their outcomes. All this could be carried out without using ICT but most stages will be enhanced and speeded up by its use. Students can become frustrated when researching and trying to contact people but the Internet and email often make the acquisition of information more rapid.

The Citizenship context might be as follows:

- School-based: how do we solve the litter problem in the school grounds?
- Locally based: how do we persuade the council to build a skate park?
- Nationally based: how can we reduce the number of homeless people?
- Internationally based: how should people in search of political asylum be treated?

Students are drawing on existing skills and developing new ones in both subjects. With the teacher acting as facilitator and providing information on a need-to-know basis, students are learning to solve problems for themselves.

Debriefing

At the end of an activity, learning is reinforced by debriefing. When there have been two sets of objectives, it is important to remember to debrief both areas. If students have been mastering a new skill in spreadsheets and exploring changes in the number of asylum seekers who have been arriving in the United Kingdom, the plenary must incorporate aspects of both to increase retention.

The balance between both subjects must be carefully maintained. This means using appropriate strategies to achieve different outcomes. Some activities, such as the development of presentations, enhance both subjects while discussion and debate are more likely to develop Citizenship skills. Equally, there will be occasions when ICT skills need to be mastered.

Building portfolios

At KS3 students' work must be assessed. An ICT input into the subject helps this monitoring process because students can record their work and build an electronic portfolio that can be used to demonstrate achievement.

Recording can take place through ICT lessons or by keeping all records on the intranet for students to access and complete at opportune moments. This is likely to be a simple tick box or brief completion of statements. It might record Citizenship activities that have taken place in lessons across the curriculum and a student's self-assessment record.

Where Citizenship is built into ICT, there is time to build a complete portfolio reflecting the work accumulated throughout the course. The portfolio will demonstrate both ICT achievement and Citizenship attainment. The process can have a motivating effect on students because of the quality of presentation and the sense of ownership they develop.

Case study: Citizenship in KS3 ICT

The school

John Cabot Technology College is based in Bristol and draws students from across the city. It is committed to the integration of ICT across the curriculum and has developed a course that combines ICT with Citizenship. The Year 7 class in the case study was just embarking on the course.

Lesson 1	Commentary
The teacher started the lesson with exploratory questioning and discussion to find out about students' knowledge and attitudes towards asylum seekers. The teacher explained that over the next two lessons, the class would be creating a leaflet aimed at providing the general public with information about asylum seekers. The initial task involved searching a range of pre-selected websites to find facts, data and images to be used in the leaflet. During the plenary, students contributed points that they considered important about the information they were gathering and therefore about the message that their leaflet would provide.	During the starter the students worked in a whole class group. Students researched the information in twos and threes. They were encouraged to discuss the relative merits of the material and images they found. Students were using a variety of software including Word, Excel and an image-handling package. The plenary took place in a whole class group and the key points were noted on the teacher's laptop and viewed on the screen.
Lesson 2	
At the start of the lesson, the class quickly listed the key factors they were planning to include in their leaflets and explained why. The core of the lesson involved further research and the creation of the leaflet. Students who completed the leaflet were asked to identify attitudes held by the general public and explain how their leaflet	The starter helped lower attaining students to focus on the message of their leaflet. The teacher moved from group to group guiding discussion and asking students about their choices. The leaflet was created in Publisher. The higher attaining students who had completed the leaflet had time for more considered discussion. Their ideas were

offered another perspective. They were to use these ideas to contribute to a presentation of their work in the final lesson.

made available to the rest of the class during the final lesson.

Lesson 3

During the final lesson, students presented their work. The leaflets were projected onto the screen and students explained their selection of material and the influence that they expected it to have. They recorded each other's ideas in order to complete a work sheet on the topic.

Their work was assessed on their appreciation of the issues relating to asylum seekers and their ICT skills.

The work was stored in an electronic portfolio.

With an interactive white board, students would have been able to contribute their ideas directly about the important factors in developing a questionnaire and the nature and sequence of questions.

Resources

The starter

The responses to initial questioning showed that the class had considerable knowledge of the issues related to asylum seekers in terms of both facts and attitudes (Figure 10.3).

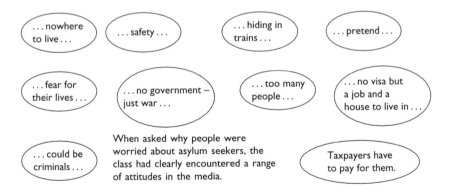

Figure 10.3

Researching the information

The students were asked to search for factual information as a basis for the leaflet. Looking for information on the BBC website proved more profitable than on the National Statistics site because of the delay in data publication.

Finding out the facts

- Why are they coming?
- Where are they coming from?
- How many are coming to the UK?
- How many are allowed to stay?
- Where do they go if they are not allowed to stay?

Some students emailed their MPs to find their views. Responses varied and gave the class an indication of the interests and views of their elected representatives.

The product

The combination of a leaflet and presentation means that the students have to justify their decisions. Making a presentation enhances Citizenship skills because students develop confidence. Members of this Year 7 class were clearly confident in speaking in front of their peers.

Reflection

The balance between the development of Citizenship and ICT knowledge and skills can often create a tension. Class discussion needs to focus on both aspects of the course. Issues relating to the use of Excel came up because the students were at different levels of attainment. It can be easy to focus on these developments at the expense of Citizenship as they come up when students get stuck. Both aspects of the course need to be made explicit in the scheme of work and lesson plans for a course which combines ICT with Citizenship. Debriefing should therefore incorporate a review of learning in both fields. It may not be balanced in every lesson because some lessons will focus more strongly on the context while others will need more attention on specific ICT skills, especially when new ideas are being introduced.

Developing Citizenship understanding

The topic provided a range of opportunities to develop a number of aspects of Citizenship in terms of both knowledge and skills. Students demonstrated their understanding of 'the diversity of national, regional, religious and ethnic identities in the United Kingdom and the need for mutual respect and understanding' combined with 'the world as a global community, and the political, economic, environmental and social implications of this'.

I want to show the conditions they live in. Can you blame them for coming over?

I want to let people know that they're not terrorists.

In contacting their MP, students are developing or reinforcing their knowledge of 'the electoral system and the importance of voting'.

It is worth noting the impact of the response from MPs. Students who received even a standard response from their MP were impressed that their missive had received an answer. A more personal response was greeted with great enthusiasm and had a memorable effect. Receiving nothing also had a memorable effect – not perhaps the one that an MP would relish!

The process of preparing the leaflet led students to think about the impact that it would have on readers and therefore to consider strategies for persuading people to read it, remember it and be influenced by its content. In doing so they were developing an understanding of 'the significance of the media in society'.

> Oh that one will make people take notice . . .

The selection of pictures featured particularly in their strategies. Emotive images such as despairing children's faces pressed against the windows of a coach were thought to be especially persuasive.

> If people take pity on the children and their parents, it will affect how they think.

Developing Citizenship skills

The activity helped students to understand and 'think about topical political, spiritual, moral, social and cultural issues, problems and events by analysing information and its sources, including ICT based sources'.

They felt that the use of ICT gave them a broader vision of what was going on and they enjoyed researching in this way. It was considered to give them access to a wider range of perspectives because

> I like finding out information.

they were looking at a range of sources. Because they had to use the information to create a leaflet, they had to consider the selection process more carefully. Students need a very clear purpose for such research or it can become very aimless. The purpose of the leaflet they were producing meant careful analysis of the information they were

> It helps us know what's going on in the world.

> We get different ideas.

looking at and evaluation of the source. After having carried out some research, they began to realise which sites provided the material that they wanted for this purpose.

> The BBC has some good stuff for our leaflet.

From the conversation in groups, the activity in school was also leading to a more informed discussion at home. Students were therefore having to justify a point of view in their home context by using evidence to support an argument.

> When my Mum said we should send them all home, I told her all about what we were doing – and that there are not nearly as many coming here now.

Not all students were quite convinced and it seems probable that some students were amending their personal view because of the environment of the classroom. On occasion, these views were expressed.

> People aren't sure about asylum seekers.

> I'm not – they kind of freak me out.

These students were having to 'use their imagination to consider other people's experiences and be able to think about, express and explain views that are not their own'.

The activity, let us hope, did something to allay these fears. The student who was 'freaked out' was later noticed evaluating images of asylum seekers in a very sensitive manner.

> This'll help people to take pity on the children and their parents.

Although the students were asked to produce a leaflet showing the facts about asylum seekers, they interpreted the activity as a persuasive one. By putting facts in front of people, they felt that it would shift some uninformed prejudices.

The production of the leaflet encouraged some of the class to 'justify orally and in writing a personal opinion about such issues, problems or events'.

Others were putting forward a case that was not their own, or presenting information that would give them a more informed perspective.

When Citizenship is incorporated into ICT, care is necessary to ensure that students are 'contributing to group and exploratory class discussions'.

The presence of computers can become the focus of the lesson and, where students are working individually at a machine, group and class discussions can become rare events. In this series of lessons, there was plenty of opportunity for discussion to take place at both levels. It must, however, always be remembered that students have two sets of objectives which must be met in an e-Citizenship course so schemes of work must be carefully constructed to achieve attainment targets in both areas.

ICT across the curriculum

Art

Research and presentations about codes and conventions and how these are used to represent ideas, beliefs, and values in works of art, craft and design.

Business Studies

ICT is appropriate for the research, production and presentation of business plans. Sites like upmystreet.co.uk provide market research information at post code level and local estate agents usually have websites which can help with the search for a location.

Design and Technology

In a topic on Structures in playgrounds and theme parks in KS3, Year 9 students can use ICT to explore the range of equipment in theme parks across the world. They can create questionnaires to discover what their peers would like to see in a playground before setting about developing their own ideas. The outcomes might be submitted to the Leisure Department at the local council to help them decide about future spending. If representatives of the council are willing to come into school, students might make presentations about their work.

English

Many activities in English make a contribution to Citizenship both in terms of knowledge and skills. They can frequently be enhanced by the use of ICT in the process for research and presentational purposes.

Geography

Students can gather, graph, map and present comparative information on the way of life in different countries and cultures and the develop an understanding of the issues faced by people in different circumstances.

History

ICT can bring artefacts into the classroom and therefore help students to develop more practical perspectives on aspects of history.

ICT

Analysing and presenting the census data in the area they live in as part of the 'Diverse Society' topic.

Mathematics

Students can use ICT to present and interpret solutions in the context of an original problem. The context for such a problem might be related to spending by the local authority, the effect on the community of building a new shopping centre or a range of other relevant topics. The outcomes can be displayed graphically.

MFL

Research and presentations comparing their culture with the country or the target language.

Music

ICT can be used to create and refine sounds representing different times and cultures.

RE

There are some excellent sites concerning Islamic pilgrimage (Hajj) and CD-Roms with interactive tours around a place of worship.

Science

Modelling the spread of disease, for example for populations with and without a vaccination programme: http://www.sycd.co.uk/can_we_should_we/explore/modelling.htm#model.

Questions for reflection

- Are there aspects of the curriculum for my subject that can be enhanced by the use of ICT and also make a contribution to Citizenship?
- What are other departments doing to use ICT to support Citizenship?
- What effect do such activities have on students?
- How can the contribution to Citizenship be made explicit?
- How can their work be incorporated into a Citizenship Portfolio?

Chapter 11

Participation in Citizenship

Why participate?

The need for participation in Citizenship provokes a range of responses from schools and teachers. Some observe that they are doing so already – which in many cases they are, as the growing number of school councils and other extra-curricular activities reflects. Others find it more difficult to deal with in the context of Citizenship. Whatever the stage of development, schools need to establish ways in which all young people can participate, reflect on the participation and have their achievements recorded, as required by the Programme of Study.

Developing skills of participation and responsible action

Pupils should be taught to:

- use their imagination to consider other people's experiences and be able to think about, express, explain and critically evaluate views that are not their own
- negotiate, decide and take part responsibly in school and community-based activities
- reflect on the process of participating.

Source: QCA Citizenship Programme of Study

Research (Hanham 2003) is beginning to show that participation offers both schools and students more than the benefits of carrying out activities with others. It gives them a sense of self-esteem and belonging which improves attitudes to school and enhances learning in other subjects.

The research examined twelve schools with a 'rich combination of participative experiences for significant numbers of students of all ages, genders, academic abilities and social backgrounds'. It explored 'associations' between participation and attendance, exclusion and overall attainment at GCSE as well as questioning heads, teachers and students.

In comparison with schools in similar circumstances the sample demonstrated better outcomes on all three counts of attendance, exclusion and overall attainment.

The head teachers all considered that 'student participation impacts beneficially on self-esteem, motivation, sense of ownership and empowerment and that this, in turn, enhances

Table 11.1 The benefits of participation

	A lot	Quite a lot	Not much	Not a lot
Made school a more interesting place to be?	34	42	21	2
	33	57	9	1
Helped you feel more confident in school?	31	51	18	0
	48	38	12	2
Helped you to concentrate better in lessons?	10	50	38	2
	11	43	34	12
Helped you to learn more in lessons?	16	41	36	6
	15	43	31	11
Helped you to work with others?	59	36	5	0
	78	20	2	0
Taken too much time from other learning?	1	1	48	50
	0	2	40	58
Worried your parents about other schoolwork?	0	0	1	99
	0	3	17	80
Made you proud of your achievements?	62	33	4	1
	64	34	2	0
Helped you to get on better with teachers?	37	42	16	5
	43	41	13	3
Caused teachers to say you were falling behind?	1	1	15	83
	0	3	11	86
Made you more interested in the world generally?	25	48	26	1
	30	54	12	4
Made you feel you can improve things?	44	47	7	2
	53	43	4	0
Helped you express yourself more clearly?	41	45	13	1
	50	45	4	1
Made you feel more independent, trusted and responsible?	68	29	3	0
	68	30	2	0

Bold = boys   Italic = girls

Source: Hanham 2003

attainment' (Hanham 2003). Teachers expressed very similar views and some gave examples of the 'transforming' impact on some students.

Table 11.1 shows the ways in which students perceived the benefits of participation. Although this research is quite tentative in that it is looking for associations rather than correlations, it appears to confirm the idea that participation makes schools a better place in which to teach and learn.

The research is a persuasive argument for governors and senior managers in search of strategies to improve their schools. It therefore gives Citizenship co-ordinators a useful tool in their armoury when discussing staffing, timetabling and budgets.

Students and participation

The longitudinal study being carried out by NFER for the DfES has questioned students on their views on participation. Table 11.2 showing 'Personal benefits of participation'

Table 11.2 Personal benefits of participation

How much do you agree or disagree with each of these statements?	Strongly disagree	Disagree	Agree	Strongly agree	Don't know	No response
Doing voluntary work may help me to get a better job in the future	6	16	51	14	11	2
Doing lots of optional activities in school may help me to get into university	5	19	46	14	13	3
Taking part in optional activities is a good way of meeting interesting people	4	8	56	19	10	3

Source: NFER 2003

Table 11.3 Personal costs of participation

How much do you agree or disagree with each of these statements?	Strongly disagree	Disagree	Agree	Strongly agree	Don't know	No response
I am too busy to take part in optional activities in school or outside	15	43	25	7	8	3
My friends laugh at people who do voluntary work	20	38	18	9	13	3
Most of my friends think that doing voluntary work is a waste of time	13	34	22	10	18	3

Source: NFER 2003

suggests that students view participation positively even if they are not altogether altruistic. Table 11.3 shows that the majority also felt that there were no personal costs involved in participating but the attitude of peers could sometimes be challenging.

Participation in practice

The range of strategies that schools are using to incorporate Citizenship into the timetable means that participation takes many different forms.

If students are to 'negotiate, decide and take part responsibly in school and community-based activities', they will be working with others in order to add value to the chosen community. This implies that they will be working with others and developing the relevant skills. All of the short-course GCSEs require students to participate in such an activity.

There are many opportunities within school to carry out small-scale Citizenship activities that help to develop the necessary skills. The following examples have been used in many schools across the United Kingdom:

- running fund-raising events such as sales and discos
- carrying out projects to enhance the environment
- working with peers and younger students in school and link primaries

- work experience
- campaigning on an issue
- involvement in school councils and other democratic organisations
- off timetable days which involve group organisation and decision-making
- running mini-enterprise activities.

Reflection is the key factor in making some of these activities genuine Citizenship activities. Students need to be able to work out the implications for those involved and how participation has benefited everyone. Running a five-a-side basketball match is not Citizenship but it is if students are able to explain that working as a group made the process more effective, that the profile of the charity has been raised by the event and that the money raised by individuals can help to make a difference.

Practical activities

A GCSE group at the Ridgeway School in Wroughton, Wiltshire:

- ran a fund-raising five-a-side basketball match
- organised a *Blue Peter* bring-and-buy sale
- made a presentation on fair trade chocolate
- taught a lesson on the political system to a Year 9 Citizenship class.

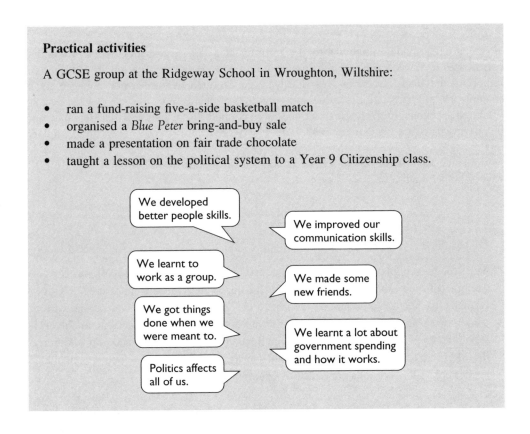

The students at the Ridgeway School learnt a lot from their Citizenship activities both in terms of skills and knowledge. The group that taught the Citizenship lesson gained understanding of the political aspects of the course as well as developing the practical skills of teaching. The groups that organised the fund-raising events started to understand how business works because they had to make more revenue than they paid in costs, consider approaches to marketing in relation to costs and organise it all effectively.

The case study shows how the parts of the Programme of Study can be integrated so students develop understanding of the course content as well as participating.

The following three examples show how activities that are to be found in many schools can be used effectively to offer students opportunities for participation.

The School Council

A growing number of schools have been setting up school councils. At best, they involve all the students in the school in discussions and the decision making process. Representatives are elected, classes discuss issues and vote on proposals and representatives feed back the outcomes and rationale from council meetings. The council must also have influence because students rapidly lose interest if they feel they are going through the motions but decisions are overridden by senior management. It is probably a good idea to define the areas of influence – with explanations for no-go areas – so decisions can be made with clarity.

A council provides insights into the running of a democratic process and therefore contributes to the knowledge and understanding as well as participation. It is therefore important that decisions are taken seriously by the head teacher and senior management if students are to appreciate the value and outcomes of democracy.

Ofsted is encouraging schools to set up school councils but concerned that they may not be offering participative experiences for all. The quote from its report shows an exemplary model.

Guidance on setting up a school council is available from School Councils UK, www.schoolcouncils.org.

Ofsted on the school council

Most of the schools in this sample have a school council, and these offer a good example of when there is entitlement for all pupils and when there is not. School councils are about representation, and have the potential to involve all pupils, who can discuss council matters in their tutor groups and elect and make accountable their representatives. In some schools the council has a very broad remit and pupils know that they have a voice in bringing about change. For example, in one school the school council activity was regarded as exemplary.

*Pupils are aware of the importance the school places on this side of its life; for example, **all** pupils recently contributed to a revision of the school code. Most of their ideas (transmitted through the school council) were accepted. The school council is active and taken seriously, as are year councils. Unusually, a small committee of pupils interviewed the candidates for the headteacher appointment last year. The successful candidate was one of the two 'shortlisted' by the pupils. This had a positive effect on the morale of the **community**.*

(Ofsted 2003)

Work experience

All schools run work experience for Key Stage 4 students. Provided that it is set up with clear Citizenship intentions, it can play a part in developing skills of participation as well as elements of knowledge and understanding.

Students can carry out Citizenship-related investigations in the organisation where they are placed. There are clear links with the role of business and the rights and responsibilities of consumers, employers and employees. The way a business deals with sustainability is also of interest. If students have placements in voluntary organisations they can explore ways in which such groups can bring about social change.

The work needs to be carefully planned and built into the work experience log. It does not have to be long but it needs to develop understanding of a particular aspect of the programme of study. The debriefing process is also important. Students will have had a variety of experiences so comparisons of the way different organisations work can broaden the understanding of a whole group. When working together afterwards, students may be able to question and challenge the way the organisation works. This is hard to do while on a placement but in the context of the classroom becomes easier.

Once complete, the investigation and follow-up work can be added to the Citizenship portfolio or log. The activity can add value to work experience by giving it a focus. Some students find themselves in organisations where few demands are made of them so carrying out an investigation can add interest.

Peer activities

Identifying opportunities in school for Citizenship activities can simplify the challenge of ensuring that all students are involved. Acting as a buddy for new Year 7 students gives both age groups a sense of belonging. The case study from Ridgeway School in Wroughton where students prepared and taught a Citizenship lesson, shows the benefits to both the teachers and the taught.

A write-up of the activity which explains the nature of the support and how it has contributed to the life of the school and the individuals involved ensures that students see participation in a bigger context and realise its contribution to Citizenship.

Such activities often make a school a better place to be and, according to research, can enhance achievement because young people develop a stronger sense of belonging, being respected and have some control over their learning environment.

Examples of peer activities

- teaching a Citizenship lesson
- working with children in feeder primary schools
- advice services for others in school
- devising anti-bullying strategies and carrying them out.

Participation for all

Depending on extra-curricular activities for the participation strand of Citizenship can lead to unbalanced provision for students because some are involved in the school council, community service and other activities while others play little or no part. Ofsted has observed that the extra-curricular route for this aspect of the programme needs careful monitoring to ensure that all students have equal access.

Ofsted on participation for all

- A failing of this strand in some schools is the concentration of experience of participation on a few pupils, without recognition of the need to find reasonable alternative provision for all.
- The issue of entitlement is of particular relevance for those schools that include citizenship provision in their extra-curricular programme. It is no doubt true that participation in extra-curricular activities can provide pupils with some of their richest experiences. These might include, for example, involvement in a national debating competition, a visit to parliament or a volunteering activity. However, some of these are available to just a few pupils, and can only be considered as enrichment. For them to be considered as part of the citizenship curriculum, equivalent activities, in the broadest sense, need to be available for all pupils.

(Ofsted 2003)

Making it work

Ofsted has observed that some schools are achieving good standards when it comes to participation. The activities do not have to be on a grand scale as the quote from the report suggests. Developing a scheme of work which incorporates a range of small scale participative opportunities is both manageable and encourages students to feel that it is not just a one-off experience but a part of life. When the Year 9 class in the Ofsted survey received a reply from their MP, they began to feel that they have a part to play in the larger community.

A range of small-scale activities that provides experiences that develop through KS3/4 lead to increasingly sophisticated outcomes through the secondary years. It also establishes a habit of participation that students will, we hope, carry into later life.

In Swindon, the local council ran an Internet-based event that encouraged students to think about its work. Several councillors put their views forward and invited students to select the individuals they wanted to keep on board until there was only one left. The 'Big Brother' strategy engaged students while they thought about the issues and became familiar with the activities of the council and councillors. With a short piece of reflective writing, the students who joined this activity have combined participation with effective learning required by the knowledge and understanding strand of the Programme of Study.

In light of the research described at the beginning of this chapter, a steady development of the habit of participation leads to a more productive school through the motivating effects on each individual.

Ofsted on participation

> Standards in relation to participation and responsible action are reasonably well developed in some schools which have considered practical and manageable ways to include all pupils in aspects of lessons or activities with a participative element. In one example, pupils in a Year 9 low-attaining class, including some with moderate learning difficulties, wrote letters to a Member of Parliament who had visited the school, asking him to support children's rights.
>
> (Ofsted 2003)

Planning for participation

Many schools have:

- incorporated the content of the course into the PSHE programme
- mapped the subject content across the curriculum and identified the contribution of each department.

Neither strategy necessarily encourages the inter-related development of the three strands of the Programme of Study. It is therefore important to ensure that the entitlement of participation is clearly present whichever strategy is being used. In Chapter 5, Rhodesway School runs Citizenship through the PSHE programme and used *The Campaign*, a participative investigation for all students. Another school that used this investigation ran it during a one-hour session every day for a week. The school does this for a week every half-term and therefore provides all students with several opportunities to participate.

In a school where each department was asked to develop a module that met the requirements of its own curriculum as well as Citizenship, the co-ordinator identified and mapped the development of participation through Key Stages 3 and 4. This was supplemented by both whole school and extra-curricular activities. A school council was established with strong class-based contributions. Students monitored their own activities and both the subject teachers offering the modules and tutors contributed feedback.

Assessing participation

All schools need clearly defined methods of assessing participation so both teachers and students know what is expected of them. Peer assessment has become increasingly established as a strategy. It works effectively when students are working together in teams and, in itself, provides a learning experience. With guidance through the early years, students develop the ability to analyse and evaluate their own and other people's contribution. In a subject that aims to increase participation in society, such skills play an important role in personal development.

Schools are using a variety of strategies to gather the information.

- Tutors keep a record sheet for each student. These are updated and discussed at regular intervals to ensure that work is being completed and problems are discovered.

- A log is kept on the school intranet so students can update their record themselves. It is then accessible to teachers who can monitor progress.
- Students are responsible for their own paper-based record-keeping.
- The Citizenship co-ordinator keeps records for all students.

Using the intranet has considerable benefits because records are safe and everyone who needs to see them has access. It also avoids keeping extensive files and means that students can update documents whenever they have access to the system. The process may be as simple as a form to complete or may allow students to upload evidence of participation and reflection on it. The development of an electronic portfolio of evidence means that students can show how their experience is growing and becoming more sophisticated.

GCSE short courses all provide a formal mechanism for assessing participation. The combination of coursework with aspects of the written paper encourages students to reflect further and apply their Citizenship knowledge to their experiences.

Ofsted has, however, observed that in some schools where GCSE Citizenship Studies are being used at KS4, the participation and knowledge strands are not being interwoven sufficiently. The tendency to regard participation as a bolt-on piece of coursework has been apparent. As experience develops, this issue will probably decline because of the nature of the assessment. The course work paperwork asks students to reflect on their Citizenship activity and the written paper provides opportunities to cross-reference the activity with the knowledge and understanding required by the specification. An Edexcel examination paper, for example, asked students to explain how democratically their activity was selected. The responses showed clearly whether a student understood the meaning of democracy and could apply it in the context of participation.

The documentation from the awarding bodies is worth looking at even in schools which do not plan to use a GCSE course because it has been set up to assess the combination of participation with knowledge and understanding.

Participation across the curriculum

Art

Enhancing the environment of a part of the school or other organisation in the community.

Business Studies

Running a school event such as a trip or a disco gives students an understanding of how a business works.

Design and Technology

Involvement in the selection of new pieces of school equipment, furniture etc. helps students to evaluate different products in a specific context.

English

Production of leaflets or other material to market the school or promote events combines National Curriculum requirements with Citizenship.

Geography

Carrying out surveys to discover how students in school and the community would like to see the local environment improved.

History

Build a picture of the changes that have taken place in the local community to create a Domesday Book or Bayeux Tapestry.

ICT

Creating posters, leaflets, marketing material for school activities. This could be combined with activities in other subject areas.

MFL

Creating information leaflets about the school or local area for foreign students visiting the school.

Music

Events designed to present music from a range of cultures combined with material to support the Citizenship perspective.

PE

Working in clubs with younger students benefits all participants.

RE

Participation in school assemblies to celebrate different religious festivals.

Science

Participation in local planning inquiries or national consultations.

Questions for reflection

- What activities are there in school that involve participation?
- To what extent are students aware of the contribution these activities make to the Citizenship curriculum?
- How might the connection between these activities and Citizenship become more explicit?
- Are students' achievements being recorded and assessed effectively?

Chapter 12

Citizenship and the whole school

Status for Citizenship

Any new subject needs to employ a range of strategies if it is to become embedded in the curriculum. Some people need to be convinced that it is worthwhile and others need reassurance that it is possible. If Citizenship is to develop the status that it deserves, co-ordinators need to avail themselves of all necessary methods to overcome people's doubts and help them to understand how the subject can enhance school life.

Citizenship champions

Having a member of the senior management team and a governor on side makes all the difference when in search of money, time and general school commitment. Research evidence (Hanham 2003) showing that there is a link between student participation and raising levels of achievement is a persuasive tool.

The senior management team is likely to welcome strategies that offer ways of raising standards. It is to be hoped that at least one senior manager has taken the subject under their wing from its inception. Involving them in activities will keep them in tune with developments. Managers are likely to welcome such projects where teachers are involved in sharing good practice in teaching and learning across the whole school.

Making an enthusiastic presentation to the governors about the development of Citizenship and the potential benefits to the whole school can be a way of identifying champions. Interested governors can be invited in for special events so they become increasingly at home with the subject and what it has to offer. Students also benefit from having contact in school with adults other than teachers.

There are plenty of opportunities for involving people from the local community in Citizenship activities with students. Working with elderly people is a popular choice but there are also opportunities with local primary schools, businesses, councillors and charities. Seeing young people making a positive contribution to the community is always welcome and may even be newsworthy. Local newspapers, radio and even television can be drawn in to let the wider community know how students are participating responsibly.

Leadership for Citizenship

The status of the Citizenship leader within a school will affect the way in which the subject is perceived. Many approaches have been adopted, some of which involve adding Citizenship to the workload of people with other responsibilities. This has both benefits and drawbacks. People with responsibilities have status within the school but many find the addition of Citizenship an extra burden and may not devote sufficient time to it. Serious time and attention need to be given to:

- identifying the nature and quality of Citizenship in existing subject programmes
- working with staff to ensure coherence between subject programmes wherever possible
- visiting lessons to help the collection of evidence for assessing students' Citizenship progress
- planning, teaching and evaluating separate Citizenship lessons with a team of staff
- planning, supporting and evaluating opportunities inside and outside of school for students' participation in Citizenship activities
- preparing and presenting reports on Citizenship policy and progress for staff, parents, pupils and inspectors.

Some PSHE co-ordinators have been asked to incorporate Citizenship into their programme. They often have the experience to work across the school effectively but it is easy to blur the edges between the two programmes in a way that leaves students uncertain about their purpose. A report on Citizenship implementation (Ofsted 2003) suggests that teams may not cover all the three strands of knowledge, skills and participation of the Citizenship programme if PSHE is the only chosen route.

A Citizenship co-ordinator who does not have other major responsibilities has the time but may not have the status to be able to influence subject leaders and year heads. Particularly in schools that take a cross-curricular approach to Citizenship, a co-ordinator without such influence may find it difficult to run the programme effectively. One new co-ordinator, for example, had difficulty persuading subject leaders to fill in the audit of Citizenship within their subjects. Fortunately one of the senior management team had become a champion and added weight to the request.

Such co-ordinators need serious support from the senior management team as well as the accoutrements that give them status such as attending management meetings and having a budget that allows interesting work to be carried out. Both these factors shift the status of Citizenship because the co-ordinator knows what is going on and can influence decisions. Participation in Citizenship can lead to changes in school routines, for example, with students engaged in more out-of-school activities or in more decision-making within school. Some degree of disruption is likely so it is important that the co-ordinator has the opportunity to explain what is going on.

Some schools recognise the scale of the job as being beyond one co-ordinator and have preferred a co-ordination team. This takes more time for meetings but involves more staff in innovation and development. It can be a good focus for a school improvement project.

Whatever type of co-ordinator or co-ordination the school chooses, the size of the budget will affect the nature of the work that can be carried out. A new specialist programme requires resources for lessons and training for staff. Student participation in school decision-making, in debates and in elections may require funds for pump-priming. The co-ordinator will also need time to set up external links with people and organisations beyond school. Without these, Citizenship is unlikely to become effectively embedded in the school routines and curriculum.

Training for Citizenship

Teaching Citizenship as a tutor or in a cross-curricular context may involve using strategies that are unfamiliar to some subject teachers.

Training, either within the school or beyond, is therefore essential if Citizenship is to be successful. The earlier chapters of this book have identified strategies that can help subject teachers to deal with uncertainty and encourage students to explore rather than expecting there to be one right answer. They have also offered questions that could be used by co-ordinators who are asked to run IN-SET within the school. They aim to help teachers identify areas of their subject which lend themselves to Citizenship and consider how they might be developed to lead students from their subject learning to developing the knowledge and skills required by Citizenship.

In-school training can help give Citizenship status, particularly if senior managers participate. It can also help to develop a co-ordinated approach across the school. If teachers are coming together to discuss their teaching programmes within and across subjects and discussing assessment, the staff as a whole will learn to appreciate their own and others' roles in the development of Citizenship. Such events can be reinforced by discussion of the benefits that the whole school can derive from effective Citizenship programmes.

> **Why training?**
>
> Some pupils are in danger of being denied the full picture since Citizenship topics need to be looked at in Citizenship ways. For any History or Geography or Maths or PE that is a school's chosen vehicle for delivering elements of the Citizenship curriculum, teachers will need to alert pupils to Citizenship concerns which may not be the same as the concerns of History or Geography or Maths or PE; these Citizenship perspectives need to be addressed explicitly – we cannot expect youngsters to have the maturity to 'make the connections' for themselves.
>
> Anthony Batchelor, Citizenship adviser to the Marches Consortium, 2003

Co-ordinators themselves often require training in order to run such sessions. There are increasing numbers of teachers emerging from Initial Teacher Education (ITE) courses who have a strong background and can support sessions. There are also Advanced Skills Teachers (ASTs) across the United Kingdom whose role is to disseminate their skills in their local area. The DfES website has a list of ASTs.

Training is available from different sources. Local education authority (LEA) advisers often run group sessions for co-ordinators. One such group is so successful that teachers meet at the end of the school day on Friday!

The Association for Citizenship Teaching website www.teachingcitizenship.org.uk has a list of training providers that includes universities which offer ITE and continuing professional development (CPD) courses, commercial providers and organisations which provide training within their specific field such as school councils.

Strategies for Citizenship

Schools have had freedom to establish Citizenship according to their needs and strengths. There is a wide variety of strategies being used. The box shows the choices being made by schools. The total exceeds 100 per cent because schools are often using more than one approach.

Current approaches to Citizenship education

Strategies	%
Citizenship-related modules or topics taught in PSHE	90
Citizenship-related topics taught more generally in other subjects	75
Citizenship-related extra-curricular activities and one-off events	57
A dedicated Citizenship slot on the timetable	15
	Source: NFER 2003

The following examples are a cross-section of those being used and many permutations exist.

The combination of teaching teams, timetabling, assessment strategies and the ethos of school and staff all influence the effectiveness of the selected approach. All strategies have their advantages and disadvantages.

Cross-circular approach

Cross-curricular

An 11–18 comprehensive school decided to take a completely cross-curricular approach to Citizenship. The co-ordinator asked heads of department to carry out an audit to see what they could contribute to the programme of study at both Key Stages 3 and 4.

Having collated the audit forms, the Citizenship programme of study was mapped across the work of departments. The gaps that were left were filled by off timetable events, and specific lessons added to the PSHE programme. Students gather evidence of their achievement and form tutors monitor it.

- means that almost every subject is involved and students can see that Citizenship is relevant to every aspect of life
- spreads responsibility for developing the programme

but

- can be hard to organise because the co-ordinator has to deal with every subject area
- can be difficult to monitor because the co-ordinator does not have time to check that subject-based teaching is making the links with Citizenship
- can be hard to gather assessment information because responsibilities are divided.

Discrete Citizenship

Discrete

The school decided to allocate one lesson a week to Citizenship. It is taught by a group of teachers who have an interest in the subject and all students take the GCSE exam at the end of Year 11.

- identifies the subject clearly
- is often taught or directed by teachers with expertise
- gives clarity for assessment

but

- can be seen in isolation from the rest of the curriculum
- does not permeate the ethos of the school.

Citizenship with PSHE

With PSHE

A dedicated team of teachers run a programme that incorporates PSHE, Citizenship and the wider key skills. The aim is to develop confidence and learning skills in a school which has a very wide ethnic mix and many students whose first language is not English.

Each class has the same teacher for the year for all aspects of the course. This gives continuity and security for some rather vulnerable young people. Assessment is carried out by each group's teacher.

- fits the timetable
- people are used to the structure
- avoids taking time from other subjects

but

- can lack definition for the subject
- can squeeze PSHE time
- teachers may not want to teach it
- pupils may not hold the programme in high esteem
- teachers who want to teach Citizenship may not want to teach PSHE.

The hybrid approach

Hybrid

The school:

- incorporates Citizenship into its existing PSHE programme
- includes cross-curricular opportunities
- runs a Citizenship week when other subjects make their contributions and special events are organised
- has a programme of events throughout the year
- offers a GCSE Citizenship studies course for students who are happy to do some lunchtime lessons to draw the rest together.

- makes the most of opportunities throughout the school
- influences the ethos of the school because staff and students are going to be in touch with Citizenship throughout school life
- provides good opportunities for active Citizenship

but

- needs careful organisation to set up the programme
- needs careful monitoring of each student's range of experiences and ensure that everyone has access to opportunities for participation.

Whatever the structure, training is an essential contributor to success. While Citizenship is clearly present in many curriculum subjects, making it explicit needs careful consideration. Teaching about slavery in History, economic development in Geography, moral dilemmas in Science or the interpretation of data in Mathematics are all the domain of subject teachers but they need help to ensure that young people make links between these topics and the Citizenship Programme of Study.

Adding Citizenship to the PSHE programme requires teachers to embrace new material and often, a new way of thinking, so they also need support. A co-ordinator may provide lesson plans but teachers need to know how to interpret and work with Citizenship ideas as they arise in the classroom to avoid students coming away with a simplistic, one-dimensional view of the topic.

There are many Citizenship resources produced by organisations with particular per-spectives, for example about multinational businesses. The resources can be attractively produced and appealing to both staff and students. Staff will need background, confidence and guidance if they are to help students to see the limitations of the materials and the perspectives underpinning them.

There are many Citizenship work sheets produced by organisations with a mission that lead to the conclusions that, for example, everything a multinational company does is wicked. Unless teachers using such resources have enough background to help students challenge the perception, there is a danger of perpetuating such ideas.

A GCSE course?

Many schools that run a GCSE in Citizenship studies view it as a way of increasing the status of a programme in the eyes of both students and teachers. Others argue that if students have to follow the programme, they might as well have the opportunity to gain a qualification. Most schools that use the GCSE route have dedicated lessons with a team of teachers who have opted to teach Citizenship as a subject rather than relying on a cross-curricular approach. One school used extra lessons on top of time in PSHE and cross-curricular work to bring students up to the appropriate GCSE standard.

The courses provide a structure for both content and skills. They set out expectations clearly and have strategies for assessing participation.

Some teachers argue that Citizenship should not be assessed in this way because the development of all students should be valued, and not just those who will get C in an examination. There is some evidence however that the participation combined with its links to the knowledge and understanding required by an exam helps some less motivated students so see the relevance of the contribution they are making.

Whichever curriculum route a school chooses will depend on the ethos of staff and students towards Citizenship as a whole and their collective views of appropriate forms of assessment.

The Citizenship team

In a perfect world Citizenship would be taught by a dedicated team of teachers who are trained and allowed time to discuss the implementation and development of the subject.

People are almost always more effective when they are teaching subjects that interest them. Strategies that expect the whole staff to teach Citizenship to their tutor group must be set up in a way that motivates them and ensures that they are well prepared. A team of staff both interested and skilled in Citizenship can lead a programme and assist more.

Running Citizenship as a carousel means that students move from teacher to teacher for different topics. If tutor sessions are at the same time, topics can be matched to the expertise of individual tutors so students benefit from their background and knowledge and increased motivation. It will also make the Citizenship element of the tutor pro-gramme more distinct as the change of teacher will give clarity.

When senior managers are involved in the team, it inevitably carries more weight in the school's decision-making process and gives status to the subject.

The organisation of the team is also important. In a school that has a group of enthusiasts teaching the subject, the team will be well defined. When everyone deals with Citizenship for their tutor group, it is essential to have an individual in a year group who is responsible for ensuring everyone knows what they are doing, is actually doing it and is overseeing the gathering of evidence. A school co-ordinator will find it difficult to manage this role across the school.

Ofsted on teams

- In one school where the teaching is consistently good, the teaching team consists entirely of senior staff who have opted to teach citizenship. Here the relevance of the subject matter and its participative style encourage a good level of motivation and a steady work rate and productivity.
- In several schools, the co-ordinator is appointed to run a citizenship 'team'. In some cases the 'team' comprises those staff who teach Citizenship, but in other cases the team comprises link teachers from subject departments or year teams. Such arrangements work well in a few instances, but in schools where the definition of citizenship is unclear, and where the team is not given firm guidance and support, the expertise of team members is wasted.

(Ofsted 2003)

Assessing Citizenship

Sunil
Citizens today need to find out the facts, consider the alternatives, weigh up the consequences, make decisions and then take action. Citizenship involves learning from the outcomes of the choices and decisions we have taken. It means being actively involved in campaigning for a fairer society.

Assessment in Citizenship gives teachers the opportunity to find out how effective their teaching has been and how students use the information and skills they have acquired. Sunil, who took GCSE Citizenship studies, had clearly developed a thorough understanding of the subject and its purpose.

A GCSE exam is just one way of assessing the programme. At Key Stage 3 records must be kept and assessments made. Schools are using a variety of methods to gather the information. The box overleaf shows the range of strategies used by teachers. The figures add up to more than 100 per cent because most teachers opt for more than one strategy.

One of the key factors that determine the choice is to keep the burden on teachers to a minimum. Some schools have come to the conclusion that self-assessment is most appropriate for Citizenship and have devised documentation to help students carry it out. It is a useful skill to acquire as it is easily transferable to other aspects of their work. They do however need guidance in making the judgements if they are to develop the ability to assess themselves effectively. As Ofsted points out, it is easy to say 'Yes, I've done it' but

Sources used to assess students for Citizenship-related topics

Assessment	% of teachers
Responses from students in class	78
Observation of students	69
Written tasks and essays	55
Group tasks	55
Students self-assess their own progress	33
Portfolio of evidence	27
Tests	19
Peer assessment	18
Other forms of assessment	8

Source: NFER 2003

much harder to decide how well and identify areas for improvement and strategies for achieving it. Working in groups or pairs is one way of encouraging young people to reflect on their achievement. Another is to provide a range of statements that students can use to decide their level of attainment.

Ofsted on self-assessment

Some schools have decided that a self-assessment element is particularly appropriate for citizenship, and have used either their own or published schemes for this purpose. A difficulty with some of these schemes is that the focus is on content coverage rather than standards and progress, although those that have developed sensible assessment criteria appear to be working more effectively.

(Ofsted 2003)

The strategy being used to teach the programme will also affect the assessment method used. If the programme is being taught by a specialist team in discrete lessons, recording is straightforward. A cross-curricular model needs more thought as information has to be gathered from across the school.

Cross-curricular modules

In a school where subject teachers are offering one module at Key Stage 3, assessment has to be in the hands of the teachers concerned. The data is then collated by the co-ordinator in order to produce an assessment at the end of the stage. The first record sheet is typical of the information that needs to be collected.

Citizen Reflection Tool

Name/Form

Module/Code

Who else was involved?

When and Where?

Description (What I did)

Knowledge Codes

Evidence of Achievement

1

2

3

4

Success Criteria (Learning Outcomes Achieved)

Negotiated

Judgement
Evidence 1 = poor   5 = excellent

Targets

Student
Signed

Date

Teacher
Signed

Date

KEY STAGE 3/4 CITIZENSHIP LOG

Name ....

PERSONAL INVOLVEMENT AND PARTICIPATION
RECORD SHEET

ACTIVITY	YOUR COMMENTS When, Where etc
School Sports Teams	
School Council/Year Council	
School Plays/Variety Shows	
School Musical Events	
Additional School Responsibilities undertaken e.g. prefect, helping at parents' evenings	
Other School Events/Trips	
Outside School Events	
Community Involvement and Help	
Other Personal Achievements	

Tutor: .... Date: ....

Cross-curricular mapping

In a less formal structure, subject teachers might record the work done by each student on the second record sheet illustrated. The class tutor then sums up with a comment for each year and produces an assessment for all of Key Stage 3.

Ofsted on gathering evidence

In one school there has already been an attempt to gather together the disparate evidence of achievement in citizenship:

> Pupils label appropriate work from other subjects as citizenship, copy it and store it in a portfolio. The citizenship co-ordinator scrutinises the portfolio and assesses it using a scale devised by the school. Pupils add evidence of work outside school, for example community volunteers and Duke of Edinburgh Award, building up a comprehensive citizenship file.

In another school a 'participation log' is used to the same effect.

(Ofsted 2003)

Ofsted on assessment

> Sensibly, some schools have begun by clarifying citizenship lesson objectives that can be assessed. Marking of pupils' work and oral comment is used to give feedback. In one school, for example, all work is marked in a conventional way with comments and grades, and this appears to be helpful to pupils.

(Ofsted 2003)

What are the outcomes?

The Citizenship Programme of Study and QCA's website lay down the expectations of a Citizenship course.

Attainment at the end of Key Stage 4

By the end of Key Stage 4, most pupils have knowledge and understanding about becoming informed citizens. They:

- demonstrate a sound knowledge and understanding of the topics and issues they have explored
- demonstrate understanding of key citizenship concepts, such as rights and responsibilities, democracy, government, fairness, justice, rules, laws, diversity, identities and communities, power and authority, sustainable development and so on, and values, for example, honesty, tolerance, respect and concern for others
- appreciate the important role and responsibility of the media in presenting information to the public and appreciate that information can be presented and interpreted in different ways

Most pupils demonstrate skills of enquiry and communication. They:

- through research and investigation of topical issues, problems and events, analyse and evaluate different sources of information including through ICT and from the media
- identify and develop questions, and consider and discuss issues, problems and events, taking account of a range of views and making appropriate use of surveys and statistics and draw conclusions
- develop and structure ideas referring to citizenship concepts and values, express, justify and defend personal opinions and contribute and respond to group and class discussions and debate
- use their imagination to consider the experiences and views of others and express and evaluate views that are not their own.

Most pupils demonstrate skills of participation and responsible action. They:

- take part in group and decision-making activities, demonstrating responsibility in their attitudes to themselves and others
- negotiate, decide and take part responsibly in school and community-based activities and reflect on and critically evaluate their participation
- communicate their findings and experiences and make suggestions for improvements and/or changes.

The evaluation from Sunil's GCSE coursework shows how he has combined the three strands of the course into his final assessment. There is evidence of knowledge and understanding, citizenship skills and participation. The group from Ridgeway School in Wroughton had taught a Year 9 Citizenship class as their GCSE activity.

Sunil – GCSE Citizenship studies – coursework evaluation

Stage 3 – To be honest, I think that my activity went quite well as we all achieved a good session with the pupils. My roles in the session were very good as I prepared some good work and made the pupils happy. I feel that the pupils got along fine with the work given and I thought they performed rather well during the lesson. I felt quite happy whilst taking part in the lesson as we all as a group helped each other and I especially went round a lot and got to know the pupils a bit. I found that they all knew quite a fair bit and that especially one boy who does not usually behave in the lesson performed very good and was no problem in the hour. Throughout the hour he learnt a lot and actually took an interest in the subject, which made us glad, as we knew he was coming involved in what was being said. Overall, I enjoyed the session with them and hope they all take part in the course next year.

I feel that especially without my other two group members, we could have not made this possible as this activity took a lot of time and preparation to organize. I feel we all did well to prepare this activity in the short time given. What I mean by this is when we found out that we could not invite an MP to come in and give a speech because it was too short of notice, we then stuck with the same idea and chose to do this 'Local government and democracy' as an activity and thought overall it went well.

I learnt a lot over the week when researching information and that the activity as a whole went well because of the amount of effort put in by us, the teacher and the students themselves. Looking back now I feel that our main aim to promote Citizenship Week was achieved and that our initial aim was also achieved. This was mainly because all the pupils took part and no one refused and that from the results etc we found out that the majority of them knew quite a bit about the topic so it became of good use to them when doing the activity. I learnt many facts about the political world and found out a lot about how things are controlled mainly by the government and by us, as citizens. I now know who does what in the government that makes key decision in how much money is spent where, who decides if we go to war, what do our local MP's hope to achieve to make life better for our County etc. All this was blank to me at first but after this I feel that I especially and others in my group and the pupils have all benefited from this activity. If I were to improve the activity, then I feel that I would find harder questions as from the results earlier I found out that a lot of people knew quite a bit on this topic. I would research better websites in order for them to research not just 2 websites but many others like it as it widens their knowledge as one could be in more depth to a particular topic. I would also see that maybe a few more could help out with the scheme to ensure that everyone who is stuck would get help and be back on task. Other things I would include are presentations etc and how I have presented everything like the questionnaires and pictures to definitely capture their interests.

Sunil's work is the product of a GCSE Citizenship studies course that is run as an add-on to the curriculum. Top-up lessons bring together the aspects of the course that is offered through distinct parts of the PSHE programme, cross-curricular contributions and special events including a Citizenship Week. During the week all subjects are encouraged to make a contribution through lessons and students put on events of relevance to the Programme of Study.

> **Making the most of Ofsted**
>
> Citizenship co-ordinators seeking to gain the leverage they will need to make a success of their responsibility across the school as a whole, would do well to remind heads, managers and colleagues of Ofsted's role. Neither Ofsted nor the GCSE awarding bodies should lead our practice in the Citizenship field. But that they are so interested in our cause must surely strengthen our arm.
>
> Tony Breslin, Chief Executive of the Citizenship Foundation, 2003

Ofsted and the awarding bodies both provide strategies for assessing Citizenship. While Ofsted will not condemn schools for not having everything in place in the early years of the subject, it will be looking for progress towards achievement of the expected outcomes.

Citizenship: the future

Bernard Crick's goal for Citizenship is . . .

> *. . . no less than a change in the political culture of this country both nationally and locally: for people to think of themselves as active citizens, willing, able and equipped to have an influence in public life and with the critical capacities to weigh evidence before speaking and acting; to build on and to extend radically to young people the best in existing traditions of community involvement and public service, and to make them individually confident in finding new forms of involvement and action among themselves.*
> (Crick 1998)

His objectives have been supported by all political parties and structures have been established to embed the subject in the curriculum. LEAs have advisers, awarding bodies have developed short-course GCSEs; Advanced Skills Teachers have been appointed across the United Kingdom, training is available from many sources and a mountain of resources is available. The growing list of good practice demonstrates how schools are showing their achievements with pride.

The continued efforts of all the agencies involved will be important for some time to come. The enthusiasm of those involved in the introduction of the subject must not be allowed to wane until all teachers and students take Citizenship for granted as an accepted part of the curriculum.

Once young people begin to feel empowered, because they have some understanding of the issues involved, they will feel more confident to make a decision about casting a vote. When they begin to feel that people will listen to them, they will feel more confident about joining in at a local or even national level. The experience of a good Citizenship programme should draw us closer to Bernard Crick's vision and help us to develop a society that gives everyone a sense of belonging and a willingness to participate.

Questions for reflection

In-school training

The source materials in earlier chapters and the reflective questions at the ends of chapters can provide the basis for an INSET programme.

Introduction to Citizenship activities – 1 hour

Teachers in mixed-subject groups meet to discuss the nature of Citizenship knowledge, skills and participation developed by the investigation in Chapter 5. Circulate the chapter before the training session.

Discussion focuses on what they think is good practice and what might be their reservations about managing such investigations in a subject context and in a separate Citizenship lesson.

They could identify opportunities for other smaller or larger-scale investigations in their own subject teaching using the Citizenship National Curriculum outline for either KS3 or KS4.

Teaching strategies – 1 hour

Mixed-subject groups could be given different chapter extracts to review different kinds of teaching strategies to develop Citizenship. Each group could be asked to develop ideas of their own for a role play, group task, etc., fitting to the school.

Sharing subject experiences – 1 hour

Subject-based groups could be convened to discuss their experiences from the first two sessions and to work on activities within their own departments. These could be developed and presented at a future meeting or be shared via school websites.

Participation – 1 hour

A final session could involve teachers working in small groups to identify possible contexts in school and out-of-school in which students could be encouraged to participate and hence develop Citizenship understanding. Chapter 11 could act as a prompt. A particular focus might be placed on how evidence of successful participation could be recorded. The ideas could be used by a team to develop a Citizenship Portfolio.

References

Ashton, E. and Watson, B. (1998) 'Values education: a fresh look at procedural neutrality', *Educational Studies*, 24(2): 183–93.

Batchelor, A. (2003) 'Are you wearing your Citizenship spectacles?', *Teaching Citizenship*, 5, London: Association for Citizenship Teaching.

Bloom, B. S. (ed.) (1956) *Taxonomy of Educational Goals: Handbook 1: Cognitive Domain*, New York: David McKay.

Breslin, T. (2003) 'Calling Citizenship to account: assessment, inspection and the quest for quality', *Teaching Citizenship*, 6, London: Association for Citizenship Teaching.

Brookfield, S. D. (1987) *Developing Critical Thinkers*, Milton Keynes: Open University.

Bruner, J. (1966) *Towards a Theory of Instruction*, Cambridge, MA: Harvard University Press.

Butler, K. A. (1998) *Learning and Teaching Style: In Theory and Practice*, Columbia, CT: Learners' Dimension.

Clarke, P. (1992) 'Teaching controversial issues', *Green Teacher 31*, Niagara Falls, NY: Green Teacher.

Crick, B. (1998) *Education for Citizenship and the Teaching of Democracy in Schools*, London: Department for Education and Skills.

Daloz, L. (1986) *Effective Teaching and Mentoring: Realizing the Transformational Power of Adult Learning Experiences*, San Francisco, CA: Jossey-Bass.

Davies, P., Howie, H., Mangan, J. and Telhaj, J. (2002) 'Economic aspects of citizenship education: an investigation of students' understanding', *Curriculum Journal*, 13(2): 227–49, http://www.tandf.co.uk/journals/online/0958-5176.asp.

Department for Education and Skills (DfES) (2003) *Teaching and Learning in the Foundation Subjects (The National Strategy)*, London: Stationery Office.

Dewey, J. (1916) *Democracy in Education*, New York: Macmillan.

Dillon, J. (1994) *Using Discussion in Classrooms*, Buckingham: Open University Press.

Driver, R., Leach, J., Millar, R. and Scott, P. (1996) *Young People's Images of Science*, Buckingham: Open University Press.

Dweck, C. and Leggett, E. (1988) 'A social-cognitive approach to motivation and personality', *Psychological Review*, 95(2): 256–73.

Ennis, R. H. (1962) 'A concept of critical thinking', *Harvard Educational Review* 32(1): 83–111.

Fisher, R. (1995) *Teaching Children to Learn*, Cheltenham: Stanley Thornes.

Fisher, R. (2001) *Teaching Children to Learn*, Cheltenham: Nelson Thornes.

Fisher, R. (2003) *Teaching Thinking: Philosophical Inquiry in the Classroom*, 2nd end, London: Continuum.

Gardner, H. (1985) *Frames of Mind: The Theory of Multiple Intelligences*, London: Paladin.

Gardner, H. (1999) *Intelligence Reframed*, New York: Basic Books.

Goleman, D. (1995) *Emotional Intelligence*, New York: Bantam.

Hanham, D. (2003) 'Participation and responsible action for all students – the crucial ingredient for success', *Teaching Citizenship*, 5, London: Association for Citizenship Teaching.

Harwood, A. and Hahn, C. (1990) 'Controversial issues in the classroom', Social science education, ERIC Clearing House for Social Studies database, http://www.eric.ed.gov.

Joyce, B., Calhoun, E. and Hopkins, D. (1997) *Models of Learning – Tools for Teaching*, Buckingham: Open University Press.

Kelly, T. (1986) 'Discussing controversial issues: four perspectives on the teacher's role', *Theory and Research in Social Education*, 14(2): 113–18.

Kibble, D. (1998) 'Moral education dilemmas for the teacher', *Curriculum Journal*, 9(1), 51–61. http://www.tandf.co.uk/journals/online/0958-5176.asp.

Kolb, D. A. (1984) *Experiential Learning: Experience as the Source of Learning and Development*, Englewood Cliffs, NJ: Prentice-Hall.

Kuhn, D. (1989) 'Children and adults as intuitive scientists' *Psychological Review*, 96(4): 674–89.

Kyriacou, C. (1997) *Effective Teaching in Schools*, Cheltenham, Stanley Thames.

Lee, H. (1960) *To Kill a Mockingbird*, Philadelphia, PA: J. B. Lippincott.

Lipman, M. (2003) *Thinking in Education*, Cambridge: Cambridge University Press.

Lynch, D. and McKenna, M. (1990) 'Teaching controversial material: new issues for teachers', *Social Education*, 54(5): 317–19.

Marton, F. (1981) 'Describing conceptions of the world around us', *Instructional Science*, vol. 10, Dordrecht, The Netherlands: Klumer,

Maslow, A. H. (1987) *Motivation and Personality*, 3rd edn, London: HarperCollins.

National Curriculum (2003) Citizenship, www.nc.uk.net.

Newmann, F. (1990) 'Higher order thinking in teaching social studies: a rationale for the assessment of classroom thoughtfulness', *Journal of Curriculum Studies*, 22: 41–56.

NFER (2003) *Citizenship: Education Longitudinal Study, First Cross-sectional Survey 2001–2002*, Slough: NFER.

Nuffield Foundation: www.nuffieldcurriculumcentre.org/go/minisite/SecondaryCitizenship.

Office for National Statistics (2001) *UK Census, 2001*, www.statistics.gov.uk/census2001/default.asp.

Ofsted (2003) *National Curriculum Citizenship: Planning and Implementation 2002/03*, London: Stationery Office.

Paul, R., Binker, A. J. A. and Charbonneau, M. (1986) *Critical Thinking Handbook*, Rohnert Park, CA: Center for Critical Thinking and Moral Critique, Sonoma State University.

Qualifications and Curriculum Authority (QCA) (1998) *Education for Citizenship and the Teaching of Democracy in Schools*, London: QCA.

Qualifications and Curriculum Authority (2002) *Citizenship: Teacher Guidance for KS4*, London: QCA.

Qualifications and Curriculum Authority (2002) *Citizenship Programme of Study*, London, QCA.

Rogers, C. (1961) *On Becoming a Person*, Boston, MA: Houghton Mifflin.

Schon, D. A. (1983) *The Reflective Practitioner: How Professionals Think in Action*, London: Temple Smith.

Schools Councils UK (2003) *Guidance on Setting Up Schools Councils*, London: Schools Council UK, www.schoolcouncils.org.

Shaftel, F. and Shaftel, G. (1967) *Role Playing of Social Values: Decision Making in Social Studies*, London: Prentice Hall.

Shayer, M. and Adey, P. (1994) *Really Raising Standards*, London: Routledge.

Slavin, R. E. (1983) *Cooperative Learning*, New York: Longman.

Soley, M. (1996) 'If it's controversial, why teach it?', *Social Education*, January: 9–14.

Stainfield, J. D. (2003) *Bihari Farmer*, jdstainfield@aol.com.

Stenhouse, L. (1970) *The Humanities Project*, London: Heinemann.

Stenhouse, L. (1983) *Authority, Education and Emancipation*, London: Heinemann.

Tear Fund (2001) *President for a Day*, Ethos Games, www.ethosgames.com and www.Presidentforaday.org.

Tipler, M. J. and Vickers, K. M. (2002) *New National Framework 7 Mathematics*, Cheltenham: Nelson Thornes.

Trollope, F. (1840) *The Life and Adventures of Michael Armstrong, Factory Boy*, London: Henry Colbron.

Vygotsky, L. S. (1978) *Mind in Society: The Development of Higher Psychological Processes*, Cambridge, MA: Harvard University Press.

Wallace, G. (1996) 'Engaging with learning', in J. Rudduck, R. Chaplain and G. Wallace (eds) *School Improvement: What Can Pupils Tell Us?* London: David Fulton.

Watson, J. and Wood-Robinson, V. (1998) 'Learning to investigate', in M. Ratcliffe (ed.) *ASE Guide to Secondary Science Education*, Cheltenham: Stanley Thornes.

Wellington, J. (1994) *Secondary Science*, London: Routledge.

Whitaker, P. (1995) *Managing to Learn: Aspects of Reflective and Experiential Learning*, London: Cassell.

Ziegler, W. L., Healy, G. M. and Ellsworth, J. H. (1978) 'Civic literacy in citizenship', in C. Klevins (ed.) *Materials and Methods in Continuing Education*, Los Angeles: Klevins.

Index